Christianity and Other Faiths
in Britain

Alastair G. Hunter

Christianity and Other Faiths in Britain

SCM PRESS LTD

BR
127
.H798
1985

British Library Cataloguing-in-Publication Data available

334 01924 9

First published 1985
by SCM Press Ltd
26–30 Tottenham Road, London N1

Typeset at The Spartan Press Ltd
Lymington, Hants
and printed in Great Britain by
Richard Clay (The Chaucer Press) Ltd
Bungay

INSCRIPTION

Make the most of WHAT YOU HAVE, ask though all seems VAIN,
ride the stormy WAVES OF DOUBT, grasp the NETTLE'S BANE;
ANSWERS you will rarely find, RIDDLES rule the WAY;
every QUESTION is a PATH toward the distant DAY.

Contents

Acknowledgments

To the word processor, whose occasionally irrational and idiosyncratic behaviour kept me mindful of the fact that nothing involving human beings has the least chance of being reliable, far less perfect.

To numerous friends, who have listened to me good-humouredly (I think!) in all manner of places, and have made more or less helpful comments.

To Eleanore, who has been both patient and generous during the writing, though never disposed to let me off lightly with idle opinionating, and who gives me hope that there are more like her, for whom this book is unnecessary.

And finally, to Jenny and Mark, who remind me that length of years is neither a necessary nor a sufficient condition for being wise.

— ★ —

Except in a few special instances, which are mostly indicated in the text, the version of the English Bible used has been the Revised Standard Version, Common Bible.

In recognition of the particular Christian meaning of the terms AD and BC, there has been a trend in recent years amongst Jewish and Christian scholars to adopt respectively the notations CE (= 'Common Era') and BCE (= Before the Common Era'). While the point may be a pedantic one, it does serve to avoid the explicitly Christian connotation of 'Anno Domini' and 'Before Christ'. I have adopted this alternative notation throughout.

Alan Race's book, *Christians and Religious Pluralism* (SCM Press 1983), came to my notice too late for it to be given detailed consideration. I have indicated in the text where it most appropriately relates to my thesis. On the whole he writes for a more scholarly readership than I have in mind, and examines a narrower field in much more detail. I find myself in broad sympathy with his arguments and conclusions, and can recommend his book highly to those who wish to follow through the theological implications of my third and fifth chapters.

Introduction

The following item was included in the January 1984 issue of *Vision One*, published by the British Council of Churches:

It was not possible to ask a question about religious affiliation in the national census, so we know how many homes have outside toilets, but not how many Hindus or Sikhs, Muslims or Buddhists or Christians there are in Britain. All we can do is make educated guesses.

* There are probably 800,000 to a million **Muslims** – mainly from Pakistan and Bangladesh, but many from Africa and the Middle East. The largest Hindu city outside India or South Africa is Leicester.
* The total number of **Hindus** is between 300,000 and 400,000.
* There are some 200,000 **Sikhs**, coming either from the Punjab and (*sic*) from East Africa.
* The **Jewish** Board of Deputies gives a community figure of 412,000.
* It is very hard to estimate the number of **Buddhists** – the Chiswick Vihara has a contact list of 20,000 and we need to remember that the second largest ethnic minority in our midst is the Chinese community, and many of the Vietnamese boat people are Buddhists.
* There are other smaller communities of **Zoroastrians** and **Jains**, perhaps 5,000 in each.
* Then there is the **Baha'i** community with 167 spiritual assemblies, with several thousand members.

The degree of religious observance is still harder to assess. It is likely that among those who feel themselves exiles in a strange land, the proportion of those attending worship will be much higher than it would be back home. But others who practised their religion in their country of origin are sometimes only too pleased to throw it to the winds when they come to Britain. There are many serious and successful efforts to win back the lapsed, to strengthen the faithful and to instruct the young in all the faith communities.

But by no means all the people of other faiths in Britain are newcomers to British society. The Jewish community has been here for a very long time, and plays a major part in national affairs. Then we have to recognize that many people have chosen to become Buddhists or Muslims, Baha'is or followers of Indian religions, even though they were brought up as Christians. No one can tell how great the influence of Yoga has been but certainly many people are deeply influenced by such a movement.

It is statistics like these which highlight the fundamental change that has taken place in British society since 1945. At the same time as the traditional Christian churches experienced a dramatic decline in numbers, the presence of considerable communities of followers of other faiths has become a significant factor. We can no longer ignore their presence, nor can we deny that in an important and irreversible way we have become a multicultural and multifaith society.

This is something which the Christian churches must take note of. If we shut our eyes to reality and retreat into a defensive mode, we will succeed only in creating a ghetto mentality and a sectarian religion of no relevance to the wider community, whose only interest will be as an object of study by sociologists in search of a recondite topic for a thesis. While that result may not be fully seen for several decades, it is already very clear that the churches' arcane insistence on the beliefs, language and worship of (at best) the nineteenth century has already greatly reduced our credibility with the generality of the population. It is perhaps symptomatic that more fuss is made by a certain caucus of literati over the preservation of the King James Version of the Bible and the Laudian Book of Common Order than over any 'real' issue. They quite clearly regard the Anglican Church at least as little better than a museum for their own eclectic interest in the outward forms of religion. This is not an isolated case. Most of us are so busy with the limited concerns of our particular church or assembly that we never see how completely divorced from reality those concerns have become. The great majority of people would hardly notice if the church went out of existence, far less lose any sleep over the matter. Until we learn to open out to a wider world, then, we are, I believe, under a sentence of death whose execution has been stayed for an indeterminate but limited period of time. One of the basic ways in which we can look beyond ourselves is to take seriously the world of faiths and try to come to terms with what that means for being a Christian today.

I would like here to quote the words of S. Wesley Ariarajah who is a Methodist minister from Sri Lanka, and is Director of the World Council of Churches' Sub-unit on Dialogue with People of Living Faiths and Ideologies:

> — The churches living in other religious cultures must theologic- ally evaluate the faiths of others, their fiduciary frameworks, and the life-affirming values in them. They cannot hold up the biblical faith as an alternative framework to organize social life.
> — The churches in other cultures need to rethink the place and role of the Bible in the context of other sacred scriptures — which are seen by others as providing equally valid guidance to organize life. They should discover ways in which their biblical faith — the faith commitment to Jesus Christ who ministered within the faith framework of the biblical world — can be held, translated and incorporated in multifaith situations.
> — The churches should ask serious questions about their relation- ship with other faiths. If it is obvious that in the foreseeable future, the only kind of meaningful national life is one which is inextricably bound up with the life of people of other faiths, and if it is also obvious that any fiduciary framework based on faith for the whole of life must be a common framework which can serve many religious communities, what does it mean for the churches' relationship with people of other faiths?
>
> It is clear that all these questions point to the need for a much fuller, more genuine and more committed dialogue between faiths. In this context questions like whether dialogue is for mission, and discussions on 'dialogue *or* mission', are out of place. In these situations dialogue is a fundamental service that we render to the community. Here, dialogue *is* mission; it is the only way in which Christians can participate and contribute to national life.[1]

This book represents an attempt to tackle the task which Ariarajah has challenged us to undertake. It is a task which I believe to be vital, which we shirk at our peril, but which opens up vistas which we can at present only dimly perceive through the mists of our sectarian prejudices. The goal is a distant one but, I am convinced, a worthy one for all men and women of faith.

Prologue

In a certain land there is a long and difficult road. Many travellers are to be found upon it, for although it holds many dangers it leads to a destination desired by many. Those who journey that way are of every type and condition of mankind. Some travel swiftly, others slowly. Some prefer the early morning, others the heat of the day; still others choose the evening or the cool of the night. They use many different maps, and take directions from a variety of landmarks. Thus those who recognize from their maps a certain distant mountain might not notice at all the stream by the side of the road which is so reassuring to others. Not a few of those who take that road are shortsighted, scarcely noticing their fellow travellers; a few are quite blind, and journey in stumbling isolation wholly oblivious to the presence of others on the road. Such conversation as takes place is mostly critical, for comparison of maps quickly reveals discrepancies as to directions and distances, and it is rare indeed for two travellers to walk together more than a few miles. Yet despite this, all who travel that road seek the same destination, though they may perceive it differently. In fact, the road both begins and ends at the common goal, so that (though they do not know it) even those travelling in opposite directions will meet at the same journey's end.

The road, of course, is life; its goal is God; and those who travel it are the children of the earth.

Addendum: One person's map

I believe that in the end human life makes sense,
and that its meaning can be found in God.
I believe that God is wholly other,
the source of everything that exists,
yet known to all who dare to look beyond their own horizons.
I believe that in Jesus, the promised One,
there is a door open to God,
a door that leads to a life of love and the giving of self.
I believe that Jesus shows me

– the oneness of God,
– the common humanity of all people
   of whatever creed, colour or race,
– and the meaning of life together.

This is my belief.

It is also my hope, and my prayer.

I

My Way

I first discovered the existence of the road when I spent three years working in Pakistan, from 1968 to 1971. Before then, like many Western Christians brought up in the ethos of the Church Militant and Triumphant, I had naively and unthinkingly assumed that, while other religions existed and no doubt had some glimmerings of the truth about them, the superiority of Christianity was somehow self-evident. But you cannot work among and with a people 98% of whom do not share your faith without *some* chink in the armour of exclusivism appearing. At least I hope you cannot. So I began then to ask some questions which have been with me ever since and which, though still far from being settled, have had a profound effect on my thinking, my faith and my life. Questions such as:

Is it necessary to be a Christian to find God?

How can we talk about the *power* of a gospel which leaves 98% unconvinced?

Does Jesus really represent God's final revelation to humanity?

Have we any right to try to 'convert' people? Surely the true calling is to all that is best in your own faith?

And so on. It may seem surprising that it should have taken a supposedly educated man so long to discover the obvious; yet it is sadly the case that there are still many who would be shocked by my even asking these questions. For too many Christians, faith is a matter of confrontation, of defending 'the truth' against an alliance of enemies and assailants, of building walls from bricks of doctrine and castles out of creeds, lest any hint of the 'other' should appear to sully the pure garments of the church. And not only for Christians.

Other religions can be just as intransigent in their insistence on being the only true and final vehicle of the revelation of God's nature and will. I refrain from naming names: as a Christian I may presume only to judge Christianity. But if the cap fits. . . .

Having raised some questions, I must make an initial attempt at answers; though at this stage I can offer only some very tentative responses. The whole book is directed towards a deeper consideration of the sort of dilemmas the previous paragraph has posed; I hope that by the end the questions at least will be clearer, even if the answers are still elusive. But for the moment, let me advance the discussion by presenting two propositions and three further questions.

    1. As a Christian I believe that God has provided us with a means of reconciliation with the divine.

    2. Other religions, using different words and concepts, have similar or corresponding beliefs.

    3. Do these different insights inevitably belong to some sort of hierarchy, with one taking absolute precedence?

    4. Can we defend the adoption of a relativist position from which we might say (for example) that my faith is right for me, while the faith of others is just as much right for them?

    5. Is it not true that we are, in different ways, engaged in the same search for the ultimate, the same quest for the source of *all* our beings?

These comments, like the previous set of questions, rather anticipate the conclusions of this investigation. For the moment they are introduced (somewhat provocatively) to set the discussion going, and to flush out into the open the more traditional assumptions that we may unwittingly hold. Whether they will survive to the last chapter remains to be seen; at the very least they serve to remind us that as believers we are not alone, that the world of faith has never at any time in recorded human history been the sole preserve of any one religion.

I have already used the analogy of the way. At the risk of incurring a charge of gross self-indulgence, I will venture another: that of *the great divide*. Most, if not all of the great religions are characterized by the idea that there is a gap, a chasm, a virtually uncrossable barrier between humanity and the divine. For the 'people of the book' (a phrase used in the *Qur'an* to describe Jews, Christians and Muslims) it is represented by sin, disobedience, and the holiness and transcendence of God. For Hindus it is expressed in the inexorability of *karma* and the fearful fate of reincarnation (it is, by the way, a typical Western misunderstanding to regard reincarnation as a blessing instead of what it truly is – a great curse). Buddhists seek the unattainable goal of *nirvana*. And Jehovah's Witnesses long to be one of the 144,000 (a figure for the number of the saved obtained by taking Revelation 7.4 and 14.1,3 literally)! This gap between the human and the divine has its tragic reflections within human society: man against woman; slave against free; rich against poor; north against south; strong against weak; East against West. And most tragic of all, the gulf between religions – a gulf that has been perhaps the most common cause of man's murderous inhumanity to man over the last two thousand years. How ironic that our attempts to close the gap between God and ourselves should have created such fatal divides between the children of that same God!

It is in the light of these divisions that I am moved to ask if we cannot progress to a more mature, more adult assessment of our various bridging techniques. If it is too much to suggest that they might be complementary, can we at least learn to see that the bridge we can cross may be impossible for others? Even more important, that insisting that our bridge is the *only* bridge may prevent many people from crossing at all? This question is made more immediate, more pressing by the fact that the world is increasingly a mixture of peoples, so that it is hard now to restrict different bridge-builders to particular geographical locations.

– 2 –

So far I have written in fairly general terms; and as long as we leave it at that level, there is no real threat present. It is possible, when the detail is not spelled out, to bask in a warm glow of brotherhood and sisterhood at relatively little cost. It is only when we get down to particulars that tension rises and arguments begin to bite. For me this has happened most acutely over the person and nature of Jesus. In the beginning the church described him as the *Messiah* (or *Christ*), by which they understood him to be the fulfilment of certain expectations in the Old Testament and in the Jewish community, a man specially sent by God, but by no means a divine figure. However, quite soon more elaborate claims began to be made, in the form of a belief that Jesus was the incarnation in human form of the divine Father, and consequently that the nature of God was multiple (in fact, threefold, allowing the further development of a divine spirit). These characteristically Christian beliefs in the *historicity of the incarnation* and the *ontological reality of the Trinity*[1] have proved to be the major obstacles to our association with other travellers on the way. Certainly we would expect different faiths to contain genuinely distinct beliefs of an ultimately irreducible character. No one human form of words can encompass more than a fragment of truth. But it is surely at these points that dialogue must take place: an *internal* dialogue to ensure that we do not preserve outmoded dogmas in irrational defiance of changed circumstances; and an *external* dialogue with other faiths, lest we should cling to our differences through prejudice rather than as part of a genuine search for a distinctive facet of the one God.

Therefore I would like to take up by way of example one issue in particular, and examine it critically to see whether, even in an area which is quite sensitive for most Christians, some sort of dialogue can take place. What follows is intended to do no more than open up the issue. I will return to it in more depth in Chapter 5.

– 3 –

Since the events of the thirties and forties, and the almost inconceivable horrors of the Third Reich, there has been a high degree of awareness of the tragic history of the Jews and the need to prevent any recurrence of such a systematic genocide. Events in Cambodia, Vietnam, Lebanon, Timor, Iran and numerous other places since 1945 show just how desperately far we are from success. Peoples are still persecuted for no other reason than the colour of their skin, their supposed racial origins, or the shape of their belief. This being so, anything that can work in the direction of greater understanding and a reduction of suspicion is worth striving for. I want, therefore, to consider in the rest of this chapter the nature of Christian interaction with Jews, and focus on the question 'Who is Jesus?'.

There is a large literature now on the subject of the Holocaust and its implications for both Judaism and Christianity. There is also a quite appropriate sense of guilt among Christians, and an awareness of the need for dialogue. But at the same time there are still disturbing signs that antisemitism is by no means a spent force. This surfaces not only in the writings of the National Front in Britain and Neo-Nazi organizations in Germany, but also in the continued acceptance in quite sober theological circles of the bias of the Gospels as fair historical comment. The Jews of Jesus' day are still for many people characterized by the descriptions given of them in the wholly subjective writings of the early church. The charge of deicide is still sometimes made against the Jews as a serious theological proposition. Now even if the Gospels were a reliable historical witness to Jewish responsibility for the execution of Jesus (and there is increasing reason to doubt this), it is a very long way indeed from the Sanhedrin of the first century to the ghettoes of Eastern Europe in the twentieth. Yet I have heard a student seriously propose that the reason for Jewish suffering throughout the Christian era can be found in their having put Jesus to death. In particular, the declaration in Matthew 27.25:

> And all the people answered, 'His blood be on us and on our children!'

Even supposing (what is unlikely in the extreme) that the crowd actually uttered these words, to imagine that they form the basis of a serious Christian theology of the suffering of the Jews is gross to the point of obscenity, an affront both to human justice and to the principles of atonement and forgiveness which orthodox Christian doctrine presents.[2]

Therefore when we who are Christian contemplate dialogue with Judaism, we must be prepared to be humble (in view of our past arrogance), to accept some measure of corporate guilt (without being neurotic about it: that would be just as illogical as blaming present-day Jews for the death of Jesus), and to recognize our status – historically, morally and theologically – as junior partners in the debate. If, given all this, we are still serious about walking the same road as our Jewish brothers and sisters, we should be prepared to consult their map. And if that means we must fold up our own for a while, so be it. In fact, if dialogue is a wholehearted engagement, there is a certain risk involved: for *we might never want to open our own map again*. At the very least, we may have to make some radical changes to it. Dare I say 'corrections'?

For example, we part from Judaism on the fundamental understanding we have of Jesus and the claims we make for him. There is nothing intrinsically anti-Jewish about calling him Messiah: a Jew could disagree with us on that point without accusing us of heresy. But to speak of God incarnate, of a divine man, and of a deity consisting of three persons – all that is to a Jew (as indeed to many others) quite outrageous. Not that *that* is in itself sufficient justification for a wholesale reappraisal. But when we note that many *Christians* have the gravest doubts about the doctrine of the incarnation; that the idea of the divinity of Jesus is inextricably bound up with the Graeco-Roman world in which it originated; and that the theological formulae of Chalcedon[3] which give formal expression to the doctrines of the Trinity and the God/man have never been popularly understood outside the context in which they were forged (if even there) – when all these points are considered, we must surely ask just what *is* it that we are defending so tenaciously? Not faith, for millions believe without benefit of much in the way of doctrine. Not the church, for it is the church which defines the teaching, not the teaching the church. Certainly not the Bible, for trinitarian belief is not to be found in it, and the notion of a God/man is at best peripheral. We may add to this the fact that no first-century Palestinian Jew could even have contemplated claiming for himself the status of a god; had he done so, he would in all probability have been lynched without even the kind of pretence at justice that is described in the Gospels.

How does this affect Christians who would engage in dialogue with Jews? I suggest that there is a *prima facie* case for investigating the shape of a christology without divinity, an account of Jesus which uses the language of the Messiah (or Christ) without deity. This would be a reading of Jesus more in keeping with his Jewish roots, and would depend on an understanding of the phrase 'son of God' along lines open to a Jew: a metaphorical expression of the fatherhood of God and our relationship to him as his children. I suspect that these would provide ground rules for a dialogue that might be very fruitful, though its results might be disturbing indeed.

This programme may seem like a selling of the pass. I hope not. I prefer to see it as a shifting of focus. Is it not possible that the historical choice made by the church in the early years of its theological development was not the only possible one? It may be that we can with profit go back to our sources, our roots, and redefine and reconstruct the way we tell the tale.

There is a famous Greek proverb: 'Know thyself'. This book is in essence a plea to Christians to know themselves, to undertake self-examination in the light of the world's faiths. Such an exercise is bound to be painful, disturbing, threatening. Things will never be the same again. They may even be better! But however difficult the task, it is I believe one that we dare not neglect if the truth we glimpse is to be shared with a world which, God knows, needs all the insights it can get.

2

Apprehensions

It is not safe to assume that dialogue is in fact an option which is recognized as an open one by most Christians. Many in the church view the exercise with extreme suspicion, or demand that it prove itself by producing converts. Even dialogue understood as a meeting with people of other faiths in order to share experiences and increase mutual understanding is often condemned. And it is not only extremists with a totally negative evaluation of non-Christian faiths who adopt such unsympathetic positions. Not infrequently church men and women of an otherwise moderate nature will react quite strongly against the thought of associating with Hindus or Muslims, Buddhists or Baha'is. Perhaps there is a latent racism at work: there is not quite the same involuntary rejection of Judaism. Perhaps there is a deep-rooted fear that the ancient certainties are being eroded, that Christian Britain is becoming a cosmoglot marketplace where those who are easily led can pick and choose amongst a hotch-potch of religions from here, there and everywhere. Perhaps it is simply the fear of the other, of not knowing where you are, which leads to a desperate attempt to put back the clock.

There is substance to these apprehensions. We *do* live in a multi-racial, multi-cultural, multi-religious society – that is true. What is emphatically *not* true is the suggestion that we can alter this, whatever may be the more or less explicit intention of the restrictive nationality legislation of the last few years. It *is* true that people today can find their faith from a wide variety of the world's religions. What is *not* true is the implication that such choosing is a careless or unthinking exercise. Many search long[1] and hard before finding God, and we merely reveal our prejudice if we condemn them because the result of their search is different from ours. Dialogue certainly *is* a risky business, as we shall see, and it will not lead to conversions. But conversion is not the only option even for Christians: *living* is a much more serious matter, and cannot be summed up in the emotional experience of a moment. If the life-experience of those whose understanding of God is other than ours can be made accessible to us, so much the better.

The purpose of this chapter and the next, therefore, is to make the case that Christians should take dialogue seriously. This is partly a response to the perceived nature of the world of faiths – to coin a phrase, can the Muslims who form 98% of the population of Pakistan all be wrong? If the answer to that question is 'yes' there are a good many supplementary problems to be faced: what happened to the power of the gospel to convince? are all Muslims eternally condemned for their lack of faith? if so, how can we talk about a God of love? and so on. . . . And if the answer is 'no', then it surely falls to us to take these people seriously, and find out what it is about their faith that makes it a clearly viable alternative to ours. If you find yourself at all sympathetic to the latter, or if you find the former hard to accept, then dialogue is an option that must be considered seriously. Let us therefore raise one more question, to test the water, as it were:

> Are there any theological grounds that would make it possible for a Christian to affirm at one and the same time the unique importance of the Christian revelation and the real and equally important insights of other faiths?

The consideration of this question, and the questions and assumptions in Chapter 1,[2] will form the background to further investigation of the nature and purpose of dialogue, and its appropriateness or otherwise as part of the Christian 'encounter with the world religions'.[3] To some, the aims of dialogue will seem perfectly obvious and straightforward. Of course we all search in our own way, and would not dream of questioning the right of others to search differently. But to many the task before us will present formidable obstacles: to those, for example, who cannot even accept as fellow Christians those of different traditions; or those who read the exclusivism of certain New Testament statements as a prescription for our own attitudes today (I am thinking particularly of John 14.6 and Acts 4.12); or those who are, quite simply, fearful of the implications of allowing the door to open on alternative – perhaps even contradictory – interpretations of the great mysteries of life.

– 2 –

In an article entitled 'The Basis, Purpose and Manner of Interfaith

Dialogue', published in 1977,[4] Bishop Lesslie Newbigin gave mature consideration to the question of dialogue as a realistic option for the Christian. His definition of what dialogue is about is worth quoting:

> In dialogue between representatives of different faiths the participants are called upon to submit their most fundamental presuppositions, the very grammar and syntax of their thought, to critical questioning. It is therefore essential at the outset to lay bare the presuppositions of the undertaking. No one enters into a conversation without presuppositions, and it is essential that these should be brought into the open. (p. 253)

Those who have been nurtured by and educated in a Christian or post-Christian society will often be in possession of a quite unrecognized set of prejudices about the inherent superiority of Christianity and the relatively underdeveloped nature of all other faiths. We have, for example, an unenviable reputation for patronizing and colonialist attitudes to those whom we regard as backward or primitive (by which, like most Westerners, we usually mean those who have not the dubious benefit of rampant consumerism). And we find it hard to imagine a deeply-held belief which does not entail some attempt at conversion. Our society is riddled through and through with the cancer of competition – and our religion reflects this: competition with God, with the devil, with our 'base nature', and with other philosophies and faiths. We are as a culture psychologically incapable of letting well alone; yet if one thing is essential in dialogue, it is that we should suspend all our tattered assumptions, and cling to one simple golden rule: the other has at least as much chance of being right as I have.

Having said this, it is interesting to see what Newbigin (a far from bigoted man) lays down as a prerequisite for Christians who would engage in dialogue:

> A Christian who participates in dialogue with people of other faiths will do so on the basis of his faith. The presuppositions which shape his thinking will be those which he draws from the Gospel. This must be quite explicit. He cannot agree that the position of final authority can be taken by anything other than the Gospel – either a philosophical system, or by mystical experience, or by the requirements of national and global unity. Confessing Christ – incarnate, crucified and risen – as the true light and the true life, he cannot accept any other alleged authority as having right of way over this. He cannot regard the

revelation given in Jesus as one of a type, or as requiring to be interpreted by means of categories based on other ways of understanding the totality of experience. Jesus is – for the believer – the source from whom his understanding of the totality of experience is drawn and therefore the criterion by which other ways of understanding are judged. . . .

The integrity and fruitfulness of the inter-faith dialogue depends in the first place upon the extent to which the different participants take seriously the full reality of their own faiths as sources for the understanding of the totality of experience. (pp. 255–56)

What is little short of amazing in this passage is the number of 'fundamental presuppositions' (I quote from Newbigin's own definition at the beginning of this section) which it contains. I shall examine them more closely in a moment; but first let me stress that there is no question of Newbigin deliberately setting up a rigid or exclusivist position, of 'manning the barricades' as it were to defend the true faith. This becomes clear when we read further and find declarations like:

Obedient witness to Christ means that whenever we come with another person (Christian or not) into the presence of the Cross, we are prepared to receive judgment and correction. . . . (p. 265)

or:

Each meeting with a non-Christian partner in dialogue . . . puts my own Christianity at risk. (p. 265)

or:

A real meeting with a partner of another faith must mean being so open to him that his way of looking at the world becomes a real possibility for me. One has not really heard the message of one of the great religions that have moved millions of people for centuries if one has not been really moved by it, if one has not felt in one's soul the power of it. (pp. 267–68)

or, quoting with approval an Indian philosopher, R. Sundarara Rajan:[5]

If it is impossible to lose one's faith as a result of an encounter with another faith, then I feel that the dialogue has been made safe from all possible risks. (p. 269)

That Newbigin still adheres to this position is clearly seen in his most recent publication, *The Other Side of 1984*. There is a particularly interesting passage which I presume tacitly refers to Rajan:

> There are many contemporary Christian exponents of the virtues of dialogue who make it clear in their writings that their 'fiduciary framework' is safe from fundamental questioning. It may be some form of idealistic philosophy, a religious interpretation which can accommodate all religions, or the 'scientific world-view', but the dialogue between religions and ideologies is conducted within this framework. It is, to quote a sharp Hindu observer, 'dialogue insured against risk'. In genuine dialogue it is the ultimate 'fiduciary framework' which is put at risk, and there is therefore always the possibility of that radical 'paradigm shift' which is called 'conversion'.[6]

There is a real dilemma here: how can we be both true to our own convictions and genuinely open to the other? The dichotomy I have identified in the particular instance of Newbigin's essay is one that is reflected in the Christian community at large, which embraces everything from the most narrowly conservative to the most diffusely liberal opinions, and all shades in between. How – if at all – can this dilemma be resolved? It may be that there *is* no resolution possible, that we must understand faith not as *certainty* but as *creative tension*: a phrase which has been greatly devalued by overuse, but which is hard to improve upon as a suggestive description of the dialectical character of the interaction of faith with life and the means of revelation. I will return to this theme in Chapter 10; in the meantime, we can use Newbigin's 'declaration of intention'[7] as the starting point for a discussion of the assumptions which we are prone, as Christians, to carry around with us.

Newbigin begins with two statements which are very reasonable: as Christians, we operate from a Christian basis; and it is that basis which shapes our thinking. But then we come to the remarkable declaration – slipped in as if it were on a par with the first two, but in reality of a different order – the Christian 'cannot agree that the position of final authority can be taken by anything other than the Gospel'. There are two critical assumptions made here without comment: (1) that 'final authority' is a meaningful concept; and (2) that we know what is meant by 'the Gospel'. Undoubtedly these are assumptions which are very commonly made. Christianity, like all the 'religions of the Book', is strong on authority, and in popular belief 'the Gospel' has almost been personified. We preach it, believe it, offer it to sinners, trust in it and sing about it; yet it is rarely defined or described. So when someone tells me that 'the Gospel' is my 'final authority' – even someone as eminent as Bishop Newbigin – I want to know more, much more!

'Authority' really needs a book to itself, so in a few paragraphs we can do no more than sketch the outline of the problem. It became a religious catch-word at the time of the Reformation, when (to over-simplify a very complex matter) the 'authority' of the church and its traditions was claimed to have been replaced by the 'authority' of the scriptures. The fact that since then the reformed churches have very largely ceased to pay any real notice to scripture, and the Roman Catholic church has become thoroughly biblical in its emphases, has done nothing to diminish the use of the catch-phrase 'authority of scripture' as a slogan characteristic of the less reflective element in Protestantism. Which is why I am somewhat disturbed by Newbigin's turn of phrase. I know that he does not mention scripture; but there is a hectoring quality to 'final authority' which I find disturbing. It is designed to foreclose the argument, and is (I would have thought) wholly inimical in spirit to the aims of dialogue.

There are two general grounds on which the concept of authority must be criticized. One is that there is a philosophical problem with the notion of absoluteness which is entailed by authority as Newbigin and many religious people define it. And the other is the practical problem that even if we accept the *idea*, it is virtually impossible to find any widely agreed embodiment of it. Every candidate for the label 'authority' known to me is the subject of such fierce dispute that it becomes ridiculous to use the term. It is a contradiction in terms to call something an 'authority' (either given or self-authenticating) which is the source of radical and protracted dispute. We end up with nothing better than a series of touchstones which are idolized by various different sects and communities in a mutually exclusive fashion. Even those sources which seem to command quite wide agreement – the Bible and the traditions of the church, for example – turn out to be chimeras. For the Bible is only as authoritative as the individual or group which interprets it – and the existence of a multitude of scripture-based sects demonstrates just how subjective a matter interpretation is. And the church has spawned in its long history so many and varied traditions that it would be possible to find grounds for just about anything at all in *that* kind of authority. These objections all seem to me to be particular consequences of the fundamental objection in principle to the very idea of an absolute or final authority. That objection can be stated thus: we are, because of our finite and created nature, incapable of expressing or understanding anything of an infinite or absolute character. Even if an absolute authority exists, we have no way of presenting it unambiguously. Whatever language we use to describe it, whatever objective model we use to symbolize it, we will be ultimately defeated by the paradox of that which is imperfect seeking to describe the perfect, that which is relative attempting to portray the absolute. It follows that the statement 'I believe in the existence of an absolute (or final, or ultimate) authority' is a classic example of an unfalsifiable statement, because 'absolute authority' is a concept which cannot be described, and is therefore impervious to any attempts to question its validity. I do not deny the possibility that some 'absolute' power exists; nor do I deny that people may believe themselves to have received guidance from it. All I wish to make clear is the logical principle that it is by definition impossible to prove (or disprove) that any particular supposed manifestation of final authority is of universal validity or application. The very statement 'I believe X to be authoritative' is itself a denial of authority!

It may be that Newbigin's appeal to 'final authority' has an emotional origin. Few of us, however intellectually rigorous we believe ourselves to be, are free from the occasional use of emotional weapons to support a weak argument or defend a prejudice. And there is no doubt that the radical openness of a genuine dialogical stance can place us in a very vulnerable position. It is tempting, then, to prepare an escape route, a last resort from which we issue the classic conversation-stopper 'thus far and no further'. I do not say that in the course of dialogue we will never reach the irreducible minimum which we find ourselves unable to abandon: all parties involved, if they believe anything at all, will inevitably reach that point – and not just once. What is fundamentally contrary to the spirit of dialogue is to decide *in advance* what that 'residue of faith' consists of. The things you imagine to be important at the outset of conversation with another rarely prove to be the real point of contact (or dispute). It makes no sense, therefore, to anticipate what can only be discovered in the course of the discussion. In any real debate, with lively involvement on both sides, the crucial questions will make their presence felt remarkably quickly. That is the point at which we have to ask ourselves what it is we are reacting to, why it is that we feel so strongly on this particular issue. And if the conversation is genuinely dialogue, we will learn (gradually and painfully) that it is here above all – when we feel most sensitive to attack – that we must keep the defences down and let the other speak in words that we can both hear and listen to. So when I hear (from Newbigin or anyone else) 'the position of final authority [cannot] be taken by anything other than the Gospel', what I hear is the sound of the defences being manned, the big guns being drawn up, the moat filling with water and the drawbridge rising.

There is another disquieting element to this declaration. We have spoken of it already, and I want to examine it a little further now. I am referring to the identification of 'the Gospel' as that final authority which must not be usurped. Something has already been said about the failure of both church and scripture to stand the test of 'absolute authority'; perhaps the expression used by Newbigin, lacking as it does the burden of several centuries of troubled history, might be sufficiently agreeable to enough people to provide a consensus. It would (of course) be neither final nor absolute: that is by definition impossible. But maybe, given goodwill all round, we have in 'the Gospel' a unifying principle, something we can all acknowledge and defer to. It will be clear from the very terms in which this hope is expressed that it is a vain one. It represents little more than an emotional desire for 'peace at any price'. At least the Bible is a serious candidate for the post of authority: given a close definition of its interpretation, it has a practical authority within a closed system. Likewise, the church as authority was highly successful when it had sanctions to back it up, whether it was the sheer physical terror inspired by the Inquisition or the subtler social ostracism exercised by the Scottish Presbyterian Churches in the heyday of their influence. But 'the Gospel' is too vague a concept to have any real clout, too bound up with the milieu of jolly chorus singing and impassioned emotional appeals from a seemingly endless succession of American evangelists. Who could take seriously as 'authority' the gospel of the born-again brigade, the shop-soiled special offers of the likes of Billy Graham and Luis Palau, Oral Roberts and Jerry Falwell?

Yet here it stands, in the sober and unemotional reflections of a man who is intellectually and morally a million miles removed from the likes of Palau. What does he mean by 'the Gospel'? Does he mean that it is some uniquely identifiable concept, presented in a form of words both perfect and immutable, so that both concept and form are fully identified? Surely not! But then its rôle as 'final authority' must be suspect; for it will be necessarily subject to the restrictions of time and contingency, in that whatever language we use to express it will be infinitely open to amendment and improvement, and therefore useless as 'authority'. Nevertheless, if we reject the charge of emotionalism, we are forced to conclude that *some* kind of permanence of expression is intended. The unavoidable implication of what Newbigin says here is that there is indeed a particular form of words which partakes in some sense of the ultimate. What he goes on to say about the nature of the gospel strengthens this impression: 'Confessing Christ – incarnate, cruc- ified and risen . . . He [the Christian] cannot regard the revelation given in Jesus as one of a type . . . Jesus is – for the believer – the source from which his understanding of the totality of experience is drawn. . . . ' The presuppositions packed into these few words are enormous; yet it is suggested that they stand as the irreducible minimum authority to which the Christian must defer. Thus we must take on board the whole metaphorical luggage of divinity, messiahship, incarnation and resurrection as a prerequisite of dialogue; and on top of that we are expected to adhere to a strong doctrine of the uniqueness of Jesus which has been expanded (in a non-orthodox fashion) into a belief that our whole understanding of 'life, the universe and everything' rests in him. It would be hard to find a single idea in that catalogue which is not the subject of controversy within Christianity, so that whatever value it may have as a possible defining creed for Christian belief must always be dependent upon an openness to other forms of expression, other metaphors. I do not wish to develop the details of this argument here: others have dealt with the problems of the incarnation;[8] I will have more to say about the divinity of Jesus and the uniqueness of his message in Chapter 5; and what is meant by 'messiah' or 'resurrection' is so much a matter of opinion that it would be hard to find even two in agreement. And the claim that Jesus is the source of our 'understanding of the totality of experience' seems to me to be little better than rhetoric. How much mathematical knowledge does our faith in Christ give us, for example?

No doubt Bishop Newbigin is concerned that we should not enter into dialogue unprepared. But the weight of ammunition with which he loads down the Christian here is out of all proportion to the task in hand. I suspect that we see here a failure of nerve: the implications of the kind of ideas expressed by Sundarara Rajan[9] will give no comfort to the orthodox, and Newbigin, conscious of this, over-reacts in order to establish his own credentials as a 'sound' Christian. I have come to believe that there is little room left for 'sound Christianity' in the world of faiths we now inhabit; and what follows will be designed to explore some of the implications of that belief.

3

Options

— I —

If it is impossible to lose one's faith as a result of an encounter with another faith, then I feel that the dialogue has been made safe from all possible risks.

I make no apology for repeating that declaration, for I am certain that it expresses the essence of dialogue. It is not something to be accepted too easily; for it poses a radical challenge to many enshrined attitudes not just in Christianity, but in virtually every devoutly held belief. Yet equally it should not be rejected out of hand, for fear of the trouble it might cause. We *need* to be challenged, to be shocked out of our complacency. Too much of our religion is rooted in the past, we still hear far too often the voice of the missionary, the propagandist (however unwitting) of Christianity's nineteenth-century imperialism carving out a sacred empire to match the secular 'Pax Britannica'. It is surely high time that we realized the world is rather more complex than the ideology of the mission field would have us believe. Hinduism and Buddhism are not going to wither away. Islam is on the march (literally and metaphorically). Judaism has emerged from the Holocaust with a stature enhanced in the same degree as Christianity has been diminished by it. And whatever we may think of Moonies, Baha'is, Hari Krishna, Transcendental Meditation and the psycho-religions of California, they are winning adherents (especially amongst the young) at a rate that ought to say *something* about the apathy, arrogance and indifference of the major Christian denominations. It is not enough to denounce the fringe groups and (in extreme cases) de-programme young and naive 'victims' of their dubious tactics. That kind of criticism is meat and drink to the persecution complex which fires every self-styled oppressed minority. (Some of

the charges made against the early Christians by their establish-
ment enemies in Rome would make the Moonies look like Boy
Scouts: yet Christianity flourished and the devotees of Jupiter and
Mithras are now somewhat thin on the ground.)

All of these factors combine to convince me that there is in the
long run no substitute for dialogue, for rapprochement, for a serious
attempt at mutual understanding. Of course the time is not right
for such a project; but then, it never will be. No doubt I stand
accused of woolly liberalism, and of a certain naivete – can you
seriously imagine *dialogue* with a *Moonie*? But if so, at least I have
an example in one who very naively said that we should pay back
evil with good, turn the other cheek, love our enemies, bless the
meek and the peacemakers, and a good many other things which
are commonly associated with the worst kind of ineffectual
liberalism. No one who founded a religion on teaching like *that*
could hope to make much of an impact on the real world! Those
who reach the point of dismantling the barricades and putting
down their weapons – the person, in short, who sees the need to put
faith itself at risk – that is the woman or man who has, I believe,
begun to reach towards the truth that Jesus himself embodied. Dare
I suggest that what Sundarara Rajan has laid down is a test of true
maturity? I believe it is, and I am certain that only on those grounds
can we hope at all to break the logjam of prejudice and bigotry
which has been the hallmark of most of our past encounters across
the religious divide.

There are in principle many different ways to approach other
faiths. Some are wholly antagonistic ('everyone but me is living in
benighted ignorance'), others wholly dismissive, seeing all religions as equally obscurantist and irrelevant. Between these two
extremes we can set out a selection of the possibilities along a
spectrum. At some point on this spectrum dialogue becomes an
option, but probably sufficiently far along to be never more than a
minority option. While statistical evidence is not experimentally
available, I imagine that a count of the number of Christians in a
population of one hundred endorsing the seven attitudes described
below would result in a fairly normal distribution in which options
(3) to (5) would cover something like 90% of the total. If anyone
would like to conduct an experiment along these lines I would be
most interested to see the results! The ordering of options in this
list may be open to discussion: it is hard to decide between the first
two as regards degree of severity; but broadly speaking the model
seems to me to work quite well. And it is, after all, only a model. No
scientific, sociological or theological rigour is claimed for it.

— 2 —

1. It is possible to hold the view that outwith Christianity all other supposed faiths are in fact mere delusions; there is no meaning, significance or reality except within the Christian community. In the Old Testament, later prophetic writing affords instances of this approach: the scathing mockery of the process of making an idol in Isaiah 44.9–20 is a particularly fine example – though whether it reflects a true understanding of how other religions regard images is very doubtful. Most thoughtful adherents of faiths in which imagery plays a central part in the expression of the deity make a clear distinction between the representation and what it stands for; and idolatry of the word has been a baneful influence in post-Reformation Protestantism. In fact it is rather rare to find this attitude clearly worked out. Most people who regard other faiths with disfavour retain an element of active suspicion and fear alongside a public posture of disdain, reflecting a lingering suspicion that there just might be something to the idols which have been held up to obloquy. Hence I have placed this as the first (and implicitly least common) option.

2. In the article referred to in Chapter 2, Newbigin makes the almost incredible remark that 'the world of the religions is the world of the demonic'.[1] While the extreme character of this statement might be lessened within the context of the full essay, it points to a way of thinking that is not entirely unknown even today. I refer to the belief that non-Christian religions are demonic in character, a source of real temptation to the faithful in that they appear to witness to truth – an appearance, however, which is intended to deceive; a deliberate and devilish ploy to trap the unwary and lead even the righteous astray. This is a regular refrain in the New Testament. Thus:

> Be sober, be watchful. Your adversary the devil prowls around like a roaring lion, seeking someone to devour.   (I Peter 5.8)

> False prophets also arose among the people, just as there will be false teachers among you, who will secretly bring in destructive heresies, even denying the Master who bought them, bringing upon themselves swift destruction.   (I Peter 2.1)

> . . . no longer be children, tossed to and fro and carried about with every wind of doctrine, by the cunning of men, by their craftiness in deceitful wiles.   (Eph. 4.14)

> Many false prophets will arise and lead many astray. . . . Then if anyone says to you, 'Lo, here is the Christ!' or 'There he is!' do not

believe it. For false Christs and false prophets will arise and show
great signs and wonders, so as to lead astray, if possible, even the
elect.   (Matt. 24.11, 23–24)

Those who hold this opinion will be especially virulent in their
opposition to all forms of dialogue, for they will inevitably see it as
precisely that subtle work of the Devil, of Antichrist, which is
spoken of in the letters of John (I John 2.18,22; 4.3; II John 7). The
attitude thus described testifies to situations of tension and
conflict, and hints at a highly defensive kind of Christianity which
was no doubt understandable at times of great persecution in the
history of the early church. But although there is some biblical
support for taking up this attitude, what ultimately condemns it is
its wholly abhorrent morality. There can surely be no defending the
belief that the God who is understood in Christianity as the God of
love should have abandoned the great majority of the human race to
the embrace of Satan, without hope of redemption, for no other
crime than having been born in the wrong place at the wrong time.
Since those who hold this dogma are often found teaching that
there are no grounds for seeing Christians as *deserving* of salvation
(everyone is equally and irredeemably sinful; only God's grace can
save anyone), it is all the more outrageous that the grace of this
loving God should be so meanly and so arbitrarily dispensed. But
then, this position is usually found within groups of a fundamentalist or narrowly conservative character, who are often as ready to
consign their less rigid Christian brethren to hell as they are to
denounce the work of the devil in the world's faiths. We must, if we
take love seriously, reject this whole approach out of hand.

3. The next three options belong to what I take to be the
mainstream of orthodox Christianity. We begin with the idea that
other faiths are by way of being a preparation for Christianity. This
may be taken on a broad historical basis – other faiths, historically
prior to the Christian faith, are imperfect adumbrations of the
perfection of Christ. Or it may be taken in terms of the individual's
history: different people pass through different faiths on the way to
full belief in the true faith. The latter is more flexible in that it
permits us to include the great religions which arose after Christianity. What it fails to explain, of course, is why some people seem
quite happy to stop at one of the preliminary stages, why others
abandon Christianity to 'go back' to another faith, and why new
faiths arose anyway, in the context of an already flourishing
Christian church. Qualifications to the main thesis can no doubt be
made to shore it up, but at the end of the day we are left with little

more than another example of a hypothesis which has died 'the death by a thousand qualifications'.[2] Nevertheless, there is no doubt that the hypothesis continues to be popular, and it too has support from scripture and from the missionary practice of the church. Paul's sermon on the Areopagus in Athens (Acts 17.22–31), in which he seeks to persuade his audience (unsuccessfully!) that their altar 'to an unknown god' is in fact a sign of the power of the Christian God, is along these lines. Much of the New Testament sees the faith of Israel as a preparation for the coming of Jesus the Christ. And within Christianity as we now know it there are many practices and beliefs which were adopted from pagan and Graeco–Roman contexts and 'baptized' into normal Christian usage. Perhaps the single most telling objection to this whole thesis is the fact that the very community which produced Jesus interpreted its own past and found continuing meaning in its faith and scriptures without benefit of any Christian beliefs. As a matter of historical fact, the continued success of Judaism means that at least one viable alternative to Christianity exists as a possible 'fulfilment' of the Old Testament. At a later stage, of course, Islam also emerged as another highly successful way of realizing the religious implications of the Hebrew scriptures.

4. The common belief that all religions have a certain amount of the truth, but only Christianity has the whole truth, represents a slight improvement on the preceding analysis. Leaving aside any discussion of the vexed philosophical question raised by Pilate, 'What is truth?', we can recognize a certain degree of good will in this approach. The preconditions of dialogue are almost present now; for there is a respect accorded to other faiths at this stage which means that at the very least there will be areas of common concern where we can treat each other with dignity. We find a hint of this approach in the story of Apollos in Acts 18.24–28 and the disciples of John in Acts 19.1–7. In each case an individual or a group of people who have already received some measure of the Spirit of God, are led into a fuller knowledge of the Christian way, after which they become effective exponents of the gospel. Paul's hymn to *agape* in I Corinthians 13 hints at the same approach, with its description of temporary prophecies and knowledge and imperfect perception, all of which will be displaced when the full revelation comes. And Hebrews suggests it in a number of places: thus 1.1–2, 'In many and various ways God spoke of old to our fathers by the prophets; but in these last days he has spoken to us by a Son . . . ', and 10.1, 'Since the law has but a shadow of the good things to come instead of the true form of these realities, it can

never . . . make perfect those who draw near.' But perhaps the best example of the concept of limited truth in other religions is found in Romans 2.14–16, where we read: 'When Gentiles who have not the law do by nature what the law requires, they are a law to themselves, even though they do not have the law. They show that what the law requires is written on their hearts, while their conscience also bears witness and their conflicting thoughts accuse or perhaps excuse them on that day when, according to my gospel, God judges the secrets of men by Christ Jesus.'

The inevitable, though perhaps unintended implication of this position seems to be that religions of lesser truth are good enough if people know no better: this is, like the previous one, a half-hearted conclusion. It fails to explain why, when the full truth is revealed, people still prefer the half-truth; and it continues to assume that 'the whole truth' is *(a)* knowable, and *(b)* enshrined in one particular human religion – both assumptions that are, to say the least, highly questionable. We have, however, advanced a little. It is no longer a matter of a linear relationship between 'other faiths' and Christianity; but instead the tentative acceptance of a *modus vivendi*.

5. We now come to what I would call the limits of orthodoxy, perhaps edging a bit over the borders! And it is here that a possibility of dialogue appears. The position about to be described is, I think, a natural extension of (3) and (4), but is the point at which many would want to pull back to a less adventurous model. It is, put bluntly, that salvation is possible within other faiths (even in the knowledge of Christianity), although it is much more difficult. There are strains and stresses involved here which form a very delicate balance. The smallest movement is enough to enforce a sudden retreat, or an irretrievable step beyond the pale. The liberal impulse sees clearly the bigotry and pride involved in making Christianity the sole effective source of salvation. But traditional teaching needs the caveat, 'It's much more difficult outside Christianity', which is as much as to say that at the end of the day only we have the right of the matter, and while other arrangements *can* be made, it must be understood that they are very much the exception! Biblical examples of this general position are understandably lacking; perhaps Paul's appropriation of Abraham in Romans 4 has some significance, particularly vv. 20–25:

No distrust made [Abraham] waver concerning the promise of God, but he grew strong in his faith as he gave glory to God, fully convinced that God was able to do what he had promised. That is why his faith was 'reckoned to him as righteousness'. But the words, 'it was reckoned to him', were written not for his sake alone, but for ours also. It will be reckoned to us who believe in him that raised from the dead Jesus our Lord, who was put to death for our trespasses and raised for our justification.

Abraham's faith *prior to his circumcision* is in this chapter presented as analogous to our faith as Christians in the God who raised Jesus from the dead. Thus Abraham is effectively classed as a Christian; or at least, as one who, within the shadow of another religion, succeeded in attaining the kind of faith uniquely characteristic of the Christian. Of course, Abraham is a special case; but we have indicated already that we are dealing here very much with exceptions. He was, in any event, a special case for many ancient writers within the Jewish community. Philo of Alexandria, for example, the great Jewish theologian who flourished in the first half of the first century CE, devoted a whole book (*On Abraham*) to allegorical interpretations of the life of the patriarch. Within the Old Testament another special case can be identified in Cyrus, the great king of Persia who defeated the Babylonians and gave to the Jews a degree of religious freedom. It is a striking fact that the only individual actually named as the Messiah in the prophecies of Second Isaiah (chapters 40–55) is Cyrus (45.1). There may be political and rhetorical reasons for this; but it is nonetheless true that Cyrus was in no sense a Jew, or particularly inclined to favour the Jewish faith (Persian policy was to allow limited freedom to *all* subject peoples),[3] yet a major prophet could envisage him as the saviour-figure who would effect the promise so powerfully expressed in 40.1–2:

> Comfort, comfort my people, says your God.
> Speak tenderly to Jerusalem, and cry to her
>   that her warfare is ended,
>   that her iniquity is pardoned,
> that she has received from the Lord's hand
>   double for all her sins.

Though possessing some degree of openness, we are as yet some way short of a wholehearted dialogical stance. And there is one further move often made at this point which, while preserving a *formal* belief in the limited efficacy of other faiths, robs it of genuine content: namely, the thesis that believers within non-Christian faiths are – whether they know it or not – in all important respects Christians. There is, in other words, a body of 'anonymous

Christians' leavening the lump of lesser religions. In Newbigin's *The Other Side of 1984* Wesley Ariarajah alludes to this device:

> In a Muslim, Buddhist or a Hindu nation there can be no question of replacing their scriptures with the Bible. At the same time one sees the need for a faith perspective and recognizes the limitations of a rational scientific framework. There are some who advocate that we identify the biblical perspectives within these faiths and name them. This is a strange solution. I have never been able to understand why a Hindu perception should suddenly become 'Christian' simply because a Christian is able to respond to it and accept it as biblically valid. Not only people, even principles can become victims of the proselytizing zeal![4]

It is hardly necessary to do more than state this belief to see its fallaciousness: if we are to resort to re-definition in order to explain all the paradoxes of the multi-religious dimension, we are no better than the priests in Lawrence Durrell's scurrilous *Pope Joan*[5] who, wishing to eat a goose on Friday, baptized the fowl as a fish before having it cooked and served! While this kind of linguistic device may satisfy the demands of a certain kind of legalism, it is fundamentally demeaning to those who are convinced adherents of non-Christian faiths: and it is, in any case, an insult to the intelligence. I would not wish to denigrate or belittle the good *intentions* that inform this position, and I think it is important to say that it does open the door slightly to dialogue. But it is none the less indicative of that defensive caution which is so characteristic of Christians, and which in its worst forms expresses itself as aggressive and exclusive dogmatism. If our faith is as strong as we insist, and the gospel as powerful, why do we so often seem to be running scared?

It will be clear by now that the dialogical encounter is a disturbing one, and that we can expect to have to give up quite a few cherished beliefs, and place ourselves in a most vulnerable position, if we are to make much of it. Furthermore, many of the representatives of other faiths with whom we seek to engage will find the exercise just as threatening, and may well retreat to entrenched and dogmatic positions at a delicate stage in discussion. We will incur charges of naivete, treachery, heterodoxy and lack of faith. Fundamentalists will denounce us, evangelicals will deny us, and the broad centre of the church will dismiss us. Little visible progress will be made, though a few individuals in each religious community may have been made more aware of the real community of faith that exists across the sectarian divides. But despite all these undoubtedly powerful deterrents, it must be insisted that dialogue is not just an option to take or leave, but an absolutely vital charge upon all who take in any way seriously the family of the human race and its relationship to God – however that may be expressed. For this reason the last two 'stations' on my spectrum, while decidedly outside the range of orthodoxy, must be regarded as the most significant for the encounter with world faiths at a truly meaningful level. They represent two metaphors intended to suggest the relationship between the many faiths the world contains. The order reflects simply my own preference, the last (not surprisingly) being that represented by the parable with which this study began.

6. The Wheel. God is envisaged as, in some sense, the 'goal' of all religions. Since, axiomatically, there can only be one God, whatever device we use to represent the religions must display them all striving towards that one end. The wheel, or circle, with God as the centre or hub, provides a quite satisfying picture. Since the figure is a circle, no one faith is better, or worse, than any other (just as King Arthur's knights were equal at the Round Table!). Since the centre of a circle is unique, the fundamental oneness of God is preserved. And since the radii are all different, they can stand for the distinctive features of the various religions. Attractive though this model may be, it fails, I think, in one most important respect: it treats the different religions as completely distinct, separate phenomena. It is as if once you have opted for one the others become quite irrelevant. The initial choice is the whole journey, and the other 'spokes' are the subject of little more than remote observation. Or, to step outside the wheel entirely, the field of religions consists of a set of discrete objects for phenomenological investigation. It may be that this kind of 'cool' approach was feasible in the nineteenth century, when Christianity was thought to have an assured place at the heart of Western civilization, and many well-intentioned people were happy to leave the other great religions in their own appointed places. The familiar situation of the colonial administrator in British Africa or India who disliked and distrusted missionaries for their unwarranted and disruptive interference in the cultures and beliefs of the 'natives' is perhaps another facet of the same attitude. Even the missionaries had their own (limited) version of this: in many places different missions (Anglican, Presbyterian, Catholic, Baptist) agreed to a division of labour on geographical grounds, with the result that to this day the Christianity found in ex-colonial territories reflects an entirely fortuitous arrangement (often depending on who got there first),

and says nothing at all about the relative merits of different Christian polities and theologies. What it *does* reveal is that from quite an early date the missionary movement was imbued with a surprisingly ecumenical spirit. It is not surprising that it was from the ranks of missionaries that the modern ecumenical movement was born in Edinburgh in 1910. However, my reservations about 'the wheel' still stand; the churches may talk to each other as much as they please, the Ecumenical Movement may flourish famously – but none of that gets us out of our own corner and into the world of faiths. To be fair, both the World Council of Churches and the British Council of Churches have in recent years been actively pursuing the question of relations with people of other faiths, in the UK especially through the BCC Committee for Relations with People of Other Faiths. But until we begin to experience the other faiths as an immediate and important dimension of *all* our religious thinking, the guidelines produced by committees will remain somewhat academic. For that reason I believe that we must move on to a more engaged allegory of the encounter of the world's faiths.

7. I need not linger long over the parable of the way. It is structured to retain, I hope, the advantages of (6) and at the same time to allow as much overlap and intercourse as possible between varieties of religious experience. Since the route is circular, the origin and goal of every religion is the same. The details of the parable provide analogies for the real differences between faiths; but the fact that we are all on the same road means (a) that the real existence of common features is expressed, (b) that opportunities are provided for sharing and meeting, and possibly increasing what we have in common, and (c) it is open to any traveller to change, to start using a different map. These factors, I would submit, reflect the realities of the religious search for many people today, and allow dialogue at its most open and most profound. But there are now no escape clauses, no safety nets. We are in God's hands alone – whatever that may turn out to mean. The scriptures are not without examples of what we might expect in such circumstances. The story of Jonah, for instance, sets out in an ironic manner the implications of taking seriously the theology of the love of God for all the world. Jonah, perhaps intended to represent the Israelites as a whole in a narrowly nationalistic mood, refuses to have anything to do with God's command that he should prophesy to the Assyrians. Not the least striking aspect of the story is that both the pagan sailors and the inhabitants of Nineveh are shown to be much more responsive and faithful to God than is Jonah: a lesson, perhaps, in the dangers of thinking that all the truth lies in one religious

outlook. A similar message, though presented in a gentler way, is found in the Book of Ruth, where the epitome of true religion is not an Israelite woman, but a girl from Moab. Many who come up against the 'challenge' of other faiths are inclined to take refuge in some of the harsher texts from scripture. Acts 4.12 ('there is no other name under heaven given among men by which we must be saved') and the stern injunctions in Deuteronomy about not bowing down to other gods are favourites. But the message of Ruth is clear: the Moabitess, too, worshipped one god; and in our increasingly small world, where religions find themselves more and more often in close encounter, it is worth bearing this in mind. 'The polemic of Deuteronomy and the "no other name" of Acts 4.12 are undoubtedly part of the Christian canon. But so also is Ruth; and we would do well to let the quiet message of that story be heard above the more strident voices of the others.'[6]

4

Theory

Many people practise dialogue without ever subjecting it to analysis. All who live in harmony and community with their neighbours in a multi-religious society are, at a basic, almost instinctive level, practising what this book is concerned to preach. Why, then, bother to preach? Why subject what is natural and instinctive to the academic mill which will grind it to nothing to satisfy mere intellectual curiosity? The reason is, of course, that instinct is a very unreliable and unpredictable guide, just as likely to lead to prejudice as to harmony. It is a wholly non-reflective process, constantly open to manipulation by knowing and un-scrupulous people. Governments and power groups throughout the world play on people's instinctive feelings to create hatred and suspicion of 'foreigners', 'the enemy', 'communists', 'deviants', or whatever in the full knowledge that they have on their side the inexhaustible force of unreason. Robert Calder expressed it well in a recent article:

> The language of prejudice is simply a way of talking which makes it possible for a group of people to sustain themselves in accepting a delusion, an illusion, and pretending that it somehow corresponds to what is in fact the case. It is a form of bullying, found usually and maybe exclusively among members of a group who have some power over the victims of prejudice.[1]

In Chapter 3 we examined a number of attitudes to other faiths. Perhaps the most common one was left unexplored: that of sheer ignorance. Most Christians know little enough of their own religion, and nothing whatsoever of any other. This may be a proverbially blissful state, but it means that any fragile harmony that develops between individuals of different faiths at a practical level is highly susceptible to the kind of manipulation referred to above. The fact that Jews in Europe had formed many social links with non-Jews prior to the Third Reich was of no advantage at all when the state prejudice of Nazi propaganda was used to give spurious justification to the 'final solution'. It is clear, therefore, that dialogue cannot be left at an intuitive level. It is too important an issue for that. Unless we have thought it through and founded it upon solid intellectual and theological principles, it will be nothing more than a vaguely nice thing to do, an extension of general good-neighbourliness. And there is nothing constant about the relationship between neighbours! Not for nothing did the ancient Israelites find it necessary to write a good neighbour clause into their sacred law (Lev. 19.18 – 'You shall not take vengeance or bear any grudge against the sons of your own people, but you shall love your neighbour as yourself: I am the Lord'). And when Jesus was asked to state the substance of the Law briefly he coupled this demand with the basic credal requirement of Deuteronomy 6.5, 'You shall love the Lord your God with all your heart, and with all your soul, and with all your might' (Matt. 22.34–40). Elsewhere, of course, he extends the principle to exclude any narrow definition of neighbour; thus Matt. 5.43 commands us to love our enemies also, and in Luke 10.25–37 being a good neighbour is defined by the parable of the Samaritan as something which goes well beyond any *natural* sense of the term. Paul too, in a passage in Romans reminiscent of the famous hymn to love in I Corinthians 13, uses this ancient commandment to emphasize the importance of love (Rom. 13.8–10 – 'he who loves his neighbour has fulfilled the law. The commandments . . . are summed up in this sentence, "You shall love your neighbour as yourself." Love does no wrong to a neighbour; therefore love is the fulfilling of the law').

With these examples before us, I would submit that a serious analysis of dialogue is an urgent necessity if we are to avoid the trap of leaving it to uninformed good will. Any such analysis will have to recognize the basic requirements of the dialogical position, as well as the essential features of Christianity. It is to be expected that tensions will arise – we have seen this already in our examination of Newbigin's article – but these should neither be ignored nor exaggerated. For they are in all probability the pivotal points for whatever new departures dialogue has to offer.

– 2 –

The fundamental nature of dialogue is [a] genuine readiness to listen to the [person] with whom we desire to communicate. Our concern should not be to win arguments.[2]

Dialogue is – conversation, not conversion; intercourse, not idle chatter; an involvement of listeners and speakers: no one who will not listen has any right to speak.

Dialogue begins when people meet each other, and never ends.

The purpose of this chapter is to set up some general principles for the guidance of Christians engaged in dialogue. It is of its nature a tentative exercise, peculiarly subject to emendation in the light of experience. I hope that what is here set forth does justice to my own perception of the nature of dialogue, and will be found to be of value by others. But there is certainly no intention that these first thoughts should represent any sort of definitive statement, even if such a thing were possible. Those who might like to explore alternative (though not wholly different) presentations will find two publications of value: the book by Paul Tillich mentioned in Chapter 2 – *Christianity and the Encounter of the World Religions*; and a pamphlet from the British Council of Churches (1981) – *Relations with People of Other Faiths: Guidelines on Dialogue in Britain*.

We begin with the philosophical prerequisites of dialogue: a series of basic attitudes which define the philosophical stance of any participant in dialogue, whatever faith they may profess. Though I have used the term 'prerequisites', I intend it to express logical rather than chronological priority. That is, I do not mean that we must all acquire this whole theoretical baggage before we sit down to dialogue – that would be arrogant and impractical – but rather that these are the principles which we will come to recognize as we engage with each other in a dialogical way. There are, I think, three categories of such presuppositions: fundamental attitudes to our own nature, to our own faith, and to the beliefs of others.

1. Fundamental Attitudes to Our Own Natures

(*a*) We are creatures of habit, mostly of habits that we do not recognize. So the first, very simple thing we have to do is to admit that fact, particularly as it affects our thinking and beliefs. Habits of mind and belief may be described as (hidden) presuppositions, the basic building blocks of our mental universe. For example, most people in the West today accept quite unthinkingly some kind of 'scientific' materialism which reduces everything that exists to atomic and subatomic particles (or, if you are more sophisticated, to mathematical equations representing forces, waves and charges). Moreover, this 'matter' is governed by 'laws' which are immutable and comprehensive; nothing happens that is not ruled by a law of science; paradox and wonder are ruled out by definition; and 'objectivity' is the key to knowledge. This is, of course, a travesty of science and scientific method, which has long since recognized the impossibility of 'objectivity' (Heisenberg), the tentative and limited scope of 'laws', and the highly paradoxical character of the basis of matter.[3]

In the same way, we come to dialogue with a baggage of 'fundamental presuppositions, the very grammar and syntax of . . . thought'.[4] We must recognize and admit this. None of us is objective, none of us has a prejudice-free outlook on life. And we certainly may not take refuge here in the supposed authority or ultimate truth of the religion we profess, as if a theory of 'final revelation' attributed to Christianity somehow protected us from the common condition of humanity. Even if it could be accurately asserted that one specific faith was in possession of perfect truth, that would in no sense guarantee the perfection of any of its adherents. Yet this is the kind of claim I hear too often from certain quarters, a claim that seeks exemption from their fallibility for all-too-fallible men and women simply because they believe themselves to have found a perfect revelation. So, at the outset, we must take the simple step of admitting that we have presuppositions.

(b) Newbigin, in the same passage, goes on to stress the importance of submitting these assumptions to critical questioning. Although this looks like a more demanding exercise, it is to some extent a natural consequence of (a). Since we rarely in fact pay any attention at all to the axioms of our thought, the mere disclosure of them is often enough to call them in question. Many men who have been unconsciously part of a male-orientated society, taking many sexist attitudes for granted simply because they are unaware of them or have never thought about them, find that the simple act of consciousness-raising is enough to call the underlying assumptions in question. Once you begin to notice the prevalence of he/him/his/man/mankind in supposedly gender-free language it is very hard to go on accepting it. The basic presupposition is called to account as a result of being called to mind. So it is with many of the unexamined hypotheses on which we build our religious attitudes. Merely to notice them is to realize that they won't bear much examination. This is undoubtedly a threatening thing, for it endangers the whole house of cards. But faith is worthless if it has poor foundations, as Paul implies in I Corinthians 3.10–15 where he argues that even if all the superstructure of the house of life is destroyed, good foundations will lead to salvation. Jesus makes the same point from the opposite analogy in the famous parable of the houses built on rock and on sand (Matt. 7.24–27). Test the foundations of your faith, in dialogue with yourself, and you will then be prepared to risk the dialogue with *other* faiths.

(c) Not only must we submit our cherished assumptions to critical self-examination, we must also submit them to criticism by others. There is no room for over-sensitivity in dialogue. We have to be able to listen when someone points out prejudice in our fundamental attitudes; and we have to be able to draw attention to the same thing in others. This is the acid test for the doctrine of 'speaking the truth in love'. If the love is lacking, what we say or hear will be resented. But if the truth is masked, a kind of dishonesty will creep into our discussions which will cloud everyone's judgment. There are no rules for this process: it is one that will grow as the relationships between the participants develop. It cannot be hurried, there are no shortcuts: dialogue is a slow growth, needing much patient nurture if it is ever to come to fruition, but affording in the end rich rewards.

2. *Fundamental Attitudes to Faith*

(a) Here I must refer again to the principle enunciated by Sundarara Rajan, and quoted in Chapters 2 and 3:[5] in dialogue, one's faith is put at risk. This is emphatically *not* to suggest that dialogue is something pursued by a crowd of spineless characters 'carried about', as Paul put it, 'with every wind of doctrine' (Eph. 4.14). Only those who recognize a strength at the heart of belief, who bring to bear a powerful sense of the compelling nature of faith, will have the confidence to run the risk of dialogue. But it must be emphasized that the risk is a real one. We engage with others whose convictions are as strong as our own, and whose grounds for belief are similarly perceived to be convincing. Therefore Newbigin's insistence that 'a real meeting with a partner of another faith must mean being so open to him that his way of looking at the world becomes a real possibility for me'[6] is at heart a demand for vulnerability in dialogue. This sounds unnatural: we are used to thinking of belief as something fixed and immovable, something hard-won and to be defended at all costs. Perhaps there is a parallel in the intellectual world. Those for whom intellectual exploration is a vital, life-enhancing concern are just as committed to, just as convinced by the conclusions they reach through long and difficult endeavour. But to abandon the exploration at that point, merely because the journey was hard, is in fact to betray the whole process. For it is of the essence of the mind to be constantly on the move: today's conclusion is the start of tomorrow's journey. Similarly, faith can never be content with 'the story so far'. What was learned in Sunday School will hardly suffice for a lifetime. The blinding discovery on the Damascus road was for Paul only a beginning. Faith, like the mind, is a restless, disturbing force – unless it is dead. The curse of the church is dead faith clothed in the faded garments of hand-me-down doctrine – and it is an all-pervasive curse, from which no denomination or sect is free. Likewise, the academic world is littered with the corpses of received opinions which carry on a shady existence for no better reason than that they are endorsed by lazy minds. Thus insistence on the openness and vulnerability of faith, far from being an unnatural demand, turns out to be of the very essence of the matter.

(b) Because of what has just been argued, one further implication must be clearly drawn and explicitly recognized. There is a genuine possibility of being persuaded, through dialogue, that the other is in important ways closer to the truth than I am. If Newbigin is right in saying that only when we have felt in our soul the power of a great faith can we claim to have really heard its message, then the risk-factor in dialogue is not to be disregarded. Nor should it be exaggerated, however: more often what will take place is some significant modification of one's own belief. Explicit conversion to an alternative faith is rare, yet it is necessary to recognize the possibility – and to welcome it as proof that we are involved with God's spirit in explorations of substantive importance for our common search. I see this as the valid interpretation of a card which Christian writers on dialogue often play: the need to witness and to be open to the power of the spirit in the encounter. Usually this is taken to mean that others might be persuaded of the truth of Christianity, and is (I suspect) designed to allay the fears and suspicions of those for whom the only proper engagement for Christians is mission and evangelism. Thus Newbigin: 'We participate in dialogue believing and expecting that the Holy Spirit can and will use this dialogue . . . to glorify Jesus by converting to him both partners in the dialogue.'[7] This is unacceptable as it stands. But when we see that it cuts both ways, that *either* can be convinced by the other, we have freed the spirit and left the dialogue open as it should be.

3. *Fundamental Attitudes to Others*

(*a*) It is essential right from the start to sit down together in good faith. We must make no secret reservations about the quality or sincerity of the other's beliefs. Whatever convictions we may have, for example, about the uniqueness and truth-bearing qualities of Christianity, it must be realized that those with whom we engage will certainly hold similarly strong and convinced opinions with regard to *their* faith. This is a point of particular importance if a dialogue is taking place in a country where one particular religious system occupies a position of recognized dominance. Thus, for all its secularism, Britain still accords Christianity a place which other faiths do not have. In Pakistan and the Middle East Islam is unquestionably dominant. In such situations those who represent the dominant faith have an added responsibility to acknowledge the honesty, genuineness and *reality* of other faiths. In certain circumstances, moreover, religions which may appear numerically insignificant carry significance and 'clout' greatly in excess of their presence on the ground. Countries which were once part of the European colonial network frequently accord such respect to Christianity, and occasionally the religion of a ruling group is not that of the majority of the population. It is clear that the prescription 'in good faith' is one that requires active attention: there are hidden political, colonialist and triumphalist factors that can, like rocks just beneath the surface, sink the enterprise of dialogue before it gets fairly afloat if we are not aware of and sensitive to their existence, and determined to steer round them.

(*b*) One of the implications of the foregoing must be that we will at all times see the faith and beliefs of the other in the best possible light. This can be a most difficult demand, for there are frequently aspects of unfamiliar religious systems that we will react very strongly against. Not that this is surprising – anyone who is thoughtful and sensitive will undoubtedly find much to question or even abhor in their own religion. What we need to be alert to is the danger of identifying what is strange with what is unacceptable. Naturally this should not be pressed too far. Dialogue is not a polite exchange of views without edge; it ought from time to time to raise hackles (on all sides) and lay siege to cherished beliefs. But it would be wrong to allow our prejudices about others ('Hindus are idolaters; Muslims are fundamentalists; Christians worship three gods; Buddhists are pessimistic nihilists') to obscure the genuine concern of dialogue to get to grips with the real content of other religions. We must therefore undertake two obligations: first, to give the benefit of the doubt at all times to those with whom we might be predisposed to disagree; and secondly, to revise the beliefs (prejudices?) about other religions that we bring into the dialogue in the light of what they themselves have to say. No Christian (to use the example of my own experience) would be in the least happy with, say, a Muslim analysis of what Christianity consisted of, if that analysis was drawn purely from Qur'anic sources. Why then should a Muslim or a Jew be expected to take seriously a Christian assessment of these faiths which drew exclusively on New Testament texts? This is a hard lesson to learn – particularly for the three peoples of the book, who are used to making rather sweeping judgments on the basis of their understanding of ancient authoritative texts. But there is a difficulty too for seemingly more open religions like Hinduism which may be effectively intolerant in their demand for an all-embracing attitude to the religions of the world. It may be easy enough for a Hindu to accept Jesus alongside a variety of other incarnations of the divine; whether this understanding of his nature would be acceptable to a Christian is quite another matter. In any case, the vaunted tolerance or openness of Hinduism can be idealized. As the tragic events surrounding the death of Mrs Ghandi reveal, deep-seated feelings of bitterness and resentment can be harboured in communities faced with what appear to be the political ambitions of the Hindu establishment in India: whatever the rights and wrongs of the matter, it is clear that Sikhs are less than fully persuaded of the tolerance of Hinduism. And periodic violence has occurred also between Muslims and Hindus (most distressingly, of course, at the time of the partition of Pakistan and India in 1947–48), showing that at grass roots level prejudice and exclusivism are no less rife in Hinduism than in any other religion. It begins, I think, to be obvious that in dialogue we subject ourselves to a most challenging and mind-stretching experience, likely to shake the very foundations of our own faith, and our apprehensions of others. The outcome may not be clear – we would not have to enter into dialogue if it were – but the journey is undoubtedly going to be a most exciting one; for instead of travelling alone we will have company on the way!

– 3 –

This book is written from an explicitly Christian perspective. I want therefore to turn now to the examination of certain theological implications of dialogue for Christianity. Once again, I must stress that what follows is more in the nature of an agenda than a set of final conclusions. Yet it would be less than responsible to avoid confrontation with certain problems which the very nature of Christianity raises, even if no satisfactory resolution of that confrontation can be found.

It will be helpful at this point to refer to certain remarks made earlier in Chapters 1 and 2. First, from Chapter 1:[8]

1. As a Christian I believe that God has provided us with a means of reconciliation with the divine.

2. Other religions, using different words and concepts, have similar or corresponding beliefs.

3. Do these different insights inevitably belong to some sort of hierarchy, with one taking absolute precedence?

4. Can we defend the adoption of a relativist position from which we might say (for example) that my faith is right for me, while the faith of others is just as much right for them?

5. Is it not true that we are, in different ways, engaged in the same search for the ultimate, the same quest for the source of *all* our beings?

Then again, from Chapter 2:[9]

Are there any theological grounds that would make it possible for a Christian to affirm at one and the same time the unique importance of the Christian revelation and the real and equally important insights of other faiths?

It is to a further development of these questions and considerations that we now turn.

In his book referred to at the beginning of the chapter, *Christianity and the Encounter of the World Religions*, Paul Tillich considers the theory and practice of this encounter. He is clear that there must be a certain exclusivism:

If a group – like an individual – is convinced that it possesses a truth, it implicitly denies those claims to truth which conflict with that truth. (p. 28)

and

Consequently the encounter of Christianity with other religions . . . implies the rejection of their claims insofar as they contradict the Christian principle, implicitly or explicitly. (p. 29)

But this does *not* automatically lead to a hardline attitude to other faiths. There are, according to Tillich, three possibilities:

(*a*) total rejection;

(*b*) part rejection, part acceptance;

(c) dialectical union of rejection and acceptance.

Of these, it is the third which is true of historic Christianity; for 'early Christianity did not consider itself as a radical-exclusive, but as the all-inclusive religion in the sense of saying: "All that is true anywhere in the world belongs to us, the Christians"' (p. 35). While this is essentially an imperialistic approach, it does at least involve a positive assessment of non-Christian religions – a minimal requirement for dialogue. Tillich concludes this aspect of his analysis by stressing the positive features of this process and using it as the basis of a dialectical relationship:

> Christianity is not based on a simple negation of the religions . . .
> it encounters. The relation is profoundly dialectical, and that is
> not a weakness, but the greatness of Christianity. (p. 51)

This principle of dialectic, together with the historical fact of Christianity's willingness to absorb beliefs and practices from others, suggests that dialogue may well be capable of being established on a sound *Christian* theological footing. I would therefore propose, as an initial statement, the following:

1. *The Principle of Respect*

We acknowledge the debt owed by Christianity to the insights of other faiths.

We recognize the validity of non-Christian faiths as bearers of truth and as revealing genuine aspects of the divine.

We note, without exaggerating its importance, the fact that in different ways there are insights shared between Christianity and other faiths.

We recognize the profound and irreducible differences between the faiths, and insist that it is no part of dialogue to reduce or disparage these.

The first of these I take to be a historical truism: both in its foundation as a composite of ideas and beliefs from Judaism and Hellenism, and in its further (and continuing) development to the present day, Christianity shows clear evidence of indebtedness to a wide range of influences. The evidence of Egyptian, Mesopotamian, Syrian, Canaanite and Greek influence on the writings in the Old Testament means that this principle is biblically founded; indeed, the Christian church adopted as its scriptures a Greek version of the Old Testament which included texts not in the Jewish canon, and which are even more strikingly influenced by hellenistic ideas. The ecumenical edition of the Revised Standard Version[10] – known as *The Common Bible* – includes these so-called Apocryphal and

Deutero-canonical books. It is quite ironical that until the Reformation they were a recognized part of the Christian canon of the Old Testament, which had never been the same as the Jewish canon. Only in Luther's time, with the introduction of the nonscriptural principle that only texts known in Hebrew should be included in the canon, were these ancient Christian texts rejected. As a further irony, in the intervening centuries several of the rejected books have now been recovered partly or wholly in Hebrew, thus reducing the reformation criterion to nonsense, and raising very serious questions about what precisely is the meaning of *sola scriptura*. Perhaps it should be amended to *sola scriptura mea*!

The second statement is of key theological importance, and is, I would argue, a necessary implication of the first: if we reject it, we are (it would seem) in the position of admitting that Christianity has been influenced by false religions. Finally, given the first two statements, the last two are required to define in general terms the relationship between Christianity and other religions.

It is often argued that Christianity is unique, and that this precludes any rapprochement with other faiths. Certain biblical texts, such as Acts 4.12 ('There is no other name under heaven given among men by which we must be saved') and John 3.36 ('He who believes in the Son has eternal life; he who does not obey the Son shall not see life, but the wrath of God rests upon him'), if taken to be the last and authoritative word on the subject, would encourage a strict definition of uniqueness. But we have already made reference to the range of influences on and attitudes in the Bible, and we have argued[11] that the idea of final or absolute authority is inappropriate for the Bible in general, far less for isolated texts within it. A simple example may suffice. There is no doubt at all that Paul understood Abraham at least, if not other major Old Testament figures, to have been saved by his faith. It is perfectly plain that the two verses quoted above fail to cover such cases, and that they are thus limited in application. While this by no means closes the matter, I hope it demonstrates that the narrow position is *not* automatically demanded from a biblical point of view. I therefore offer as a second principle the following:

2. *The Principle of Uniqueness*

Certain fundamental doctrines or beliefs of Christianity are unique to that faith.

These are the beliefs which are essential to Christianity and which define its particular appeal.

We recognize that other religious systems also present unique beliefs which similarly constitute the character and appeal of these faiths.

No attempt is made here either to spell out any details of the 'fundamental doctrines of Christianity' or to compare the qualities of different faiths. Something will be said on the former in Chapter 6; the latter is taken up in the third principle, below. For the moment, I simply present the second principle as it stands, a relatively non-controversial statement of the actual conditions which define and differentiate religions.

One further statement is required. We have so far avoided the crucial questions of the priority, truth content, and value of different faiths. The narrow position simply asserts that only Christianity has any truth or value, and so the uniqueness of other religions can be dismissed as the uniqueness of error. Most would hesitate to be so sweeping in judgment, and would wish to accord some sort of validity to the insights of the non-Christian systems. In that case, the problem of priorities, of some kind of hierarchy of the world's religions becomes acute. Few would go so far as to attempt any comprehensive ordering, though many popular (Christian) accounts in the past have begun with so-called 'primitive' systems ('Animism'), have moved on to cyclical, polytheistic and pantheistic systems (Ancient Greek and Roman; Hindu), thence to 'historical' religions (Judaism and Islam), and finally to the 'truth' (Christianity). It is beyond the scope of the present work to analyse this presentation: its flaws are manifold. Perhaps I may be permitted just one observation. It is tacitly assumed that those religions which claim to be 'historical' are the most advanced. Yet it could with some justification be argued that it is these same religions which have, in their desire to control history, spilled most innocent blood in the name of faith; an assessment which must seriously undermine any claim they may have to the description 'advanced'. this leads me, then, to my third and most clearly controversial principle:

3. *The Principle of Relativity*

No arrangement of religious systems according to priority of truth, value, knowledge of God or efficacy for salvation can be made.

Notwithstanding, the adherent of any one faith may assert with complete sincerity that his or her faith is the only 'true' faith (where 'true' may be replaced by any other expression which is felt to be appropriate).

No single religion possesses a complete understanding of God, nor can any single religion claim to be or to have the last word of revelation.

The middle one of these three assertions looks out of place. However, it is included here because it is undoubtedly the way many, if not most believers would choose to express their faith – *whatever that faith may be*. This being so, there is a built-in relativity to such assertions. They always include the unspoken but necessary qualification 'for me', and so belong properly with the third principle. One of the aims of dialogue is that we should at some point come to recognize that qualification, and welcome it. For this recognition is a mark of 'coming of age' in the encounter between faiths. The other two assertions require no further elucidation here. They have been essentially dealt with in Chapter 3, and are of the absolute essence of dialogue understood as a meeting between human beings who, recognizing their human imperfections, strive together to reach the divine and to explore the many ways in which the divine has reached down to humankind.

5

Exemplar

— I —

In Chapter 1,[1] we raised the familiar question, 'Who is Jesus?' in order to illustrate the kind of inner dialogue that might be entailed by the encounter of Christianity with other faiths, and in particular, by the engagement with Judaism. The possibility was introduced of developing a 'christology without divinity'. In Chapter 4[2] we noted the existence of certain fundamental beliefs by which any faith may be uniquely characterized. It will be necessary in due course to essay a general description of the defining beliefs of Christianity; but before doing so, I would like to take one case study in particular, by presenting a discussion of the nature of Jesus in which some of the usual Christian presuppositions are questioned.

To a great extent our understanding of the nature of Jesus has been conditioned by certain theological axioms. Whatever the historical value of the concept of 'the divine man', it has become a theological necessity: the assumptions we want to make about the efficacy of Christianity demand that Jesus be divine. This has had a curious effect on the historical judgment of otherwise reputable scholars, whose confessional status frequently forces them into a rejection of historical conclusions about Jesus not because they are improbable, but because they are unacceptable. I have heard Catholic and Orthodox scholars insist that the virgin birth and the incarnation must be accepted as historical facts, *even in the face of wholly antagonistic evidence* because the doctrine of the nature of Jesus demands it. As a teacher in a Divinity Faculty I regularly find that candidates for the Christian ministry, who see the force of many critical arguments about the biblical materials while students, consciously reject them on accepting a charge, on the grounds that their congregations will be unable to cope with such 'dangerous' thought! I find this kind of self-censorship profoundly disturbing. Sometimes it is a question of job-preservation, in which case it is understandable though despicable. But more often it appears to reflect a real schizophrenia of attitude in which all evidence is subjected to a strange kind of truth test: only that which supports the presupposed system of beliefs is admitted publicly, although doubts may be expressed in private. This is by no means limited to the clergy. The ranks of fundamentalism and conservative evangelicalism contain many who are first-class scholars in their own discipline (frequently medicine or one of the sciences), but who display a level of credulity with regard to theology and scripture which would make them a laughing stock in their own field. Worse still – and particularly unforgivable in a scholarly community – they arrogantly reject the studies and conclusions of those who *are* acknowledged experts in these areas.

It is surely insulting to the intelligence and the faith of congregations thus to censor what they may hear: it is unlikely that faith worthy of the name is such a delicate growth as to require to be sheltered from the cold winds of academic reflection! Perhaps, though, censorship is more often a matter of self-preservation. Priests or preachers, afflicted themselves by doubts, take avoiding action and hope the problem will go away. But of course this is a counsel of desperation which ultimately takes its toll in the form either of increasing disillusion, or of a retreat from all thought into a rigid orthodoxy which admits no questions because it claims to know all the answers. In each case those who seek are sent away empty-handed and disappointed, either by the cynicism of the first or the shallow dogmatism of the second, and the faith that was meant to be preserved is effectively destroyed. It is my contention that a lively mind attended by a strong faith can, through interior and exterior dialogue, build a strong and lasting house in which to dwell.

– 2 –

Something needs to be said about the presuppositions – so often unexamined – that lead to the popular picture of Jesus the divine king, born on earth but fathered by God, a Jesus very far removed from the low-class Jew who made his mark in Galilee and Judaea in the first century. Anselm, many centuries ago, wrote a treatise on the nature of Christ under the title *Cur Deus Homo?* ('Why the God-man?'). We need to ask, not *why* but *whence* the 'God-man'.

When Christianity and Judaism were developing their character-

istic forms, in the first century CE, doctrines new to the Jewish
thought world, such as the belief in resurrection and life after death,
were opening up possibilities for theology that were not available to
most of the Old Testament writers. Other themes, like the old
Canaanite myths of conflict between God and the forces of chaos,
and Persian belief in a dualistic struggle between the principles of
good and evil which was carried on simultaneously in the heavenly
and the earthly spheres, provided a set of concepts and metaphors
with which to tackle the age-old problem of why the good suffer and
the wicked flourish. The earliest result was what we now call
apocalyptic literature, of which the best biblical examples are the
second half of Daniel (chapters 7 to 12) in the Old Testament, and
the Book of Revelation in the New. One of the key features of this
genre of writing was the belief that the created order had become
fundamentally corrupt, together with a corresponding expectation
that at the end of time God would destroy everything and bring in a
new creation and a new world order. At the same time an increasing
place was given to figures whose function was to mediate between
the transcendent God and his creation, and the revelation of the
secrets of the last age was always supposed to have been made by
means of an individual of some standing from the past. Thus
Daniel, whose historical location is *c*.550 BCE, is presented as the
source of the visions in the book named after him, which was in
fact written about 165 BCE. Outside the Old Testament canon we
find apocalyptic books attributed to Enoch (see Gen. 5.21–24),
Abraham, Adam, Baruch, Daniel, Elijah and Ezra, and ranging over
a period from the second century BCE to the third century CE. The
Book of Revelation speaks of John as the recipient of its visions, and
Christian tradition identified him with John the Apostle, on the
same general principle. Besides these earthly (or perhaps superhu-
man) recipients of revelation, there was a panoply of semi-divine
beings, angels with specific responsibilities. Daniel and Revelation
both provide evidence of this development. And lastly, several
works introduce a supreme mediator who bears a very close
relationship to the Almighty. He is not identified with God; if a
contemporary analogy were to be drawn, he might be described as
God's personal assistant, his 'right hand man'. His responsibilities
included the dispensation of justice on the day of judgment, and
hosting the great banquet to be shared by the righteous. In Enoch he
is described as 'the Elect One' and 'the Son of Man'; Daniel 7.13
speaks of 'one like a son of man' who is given dominion over the
nations – almost certainly an angelic figure; and in Revelation we
find the same role given to the Lamb of God.

Out of this melting pot two fundamental beliefs entered Christianity: the corruption of humankind, and the need for a mediator between God and his creation. As long as the first of these is understood as metaphor or rhetoric it is a serviceable account of a common, though not universal, perception of the nature of humanity. And the second represents the strong feeling that God as a transcendent being could not under any circumstances be immediately apprehended by mere human beings. In the centuries before Jesus, popular piety peopled heaven with a variety of angels who acted as God's messengers to men and women: the use Luke makes of angels in his account of the birth of Jesus is an excellent example of this. Jewish philosophical theology introduced such ideas as the *logos* (Philo of Alexandria), or a personification of *Wisdom* (Ecclesiasticus). These last two developments were so important for later thinking about God within Christianity that some further explanation of them would not go amiss.

As early as Proverbs chapter 8 we find a Hebrew writer presenting the figure of Wisdom personified (as a female!). Thus, in vv. 22–31:

> Yahweh created me at the beginning of his work,
>   the first of his acts of old.
> Ages ago I was set up,
>   at the first, before the beginning of the earth.
>
>   ....
>
> When he established the heavens, I was there,
>   when he drew a circle on the face of the deep,
> when he made firm the skies above,
>   when he established the fountains of the deep
>
>   ....
>
>   then I was beside him, like a master workman;
> and I was daily his delight,
>   rejoicing before him always,
> rejoicing in his inhabited world
>   and delighting in the sons of men.

Ecclesiasticus (also known by the writer's personal name, Jesus Ben Sira), writing about 180 BCE, goes still further, in chapter 24.3–7, where once again Wisdom is a female figure:

> [Wisdom is speaking]
> I came forth from the mouth of the Most High,
>   and covered the earth like a mist.

> I dwelt in high places,
>> and my throne was in a pillar of cloud.
> Alone I have made the circuit of the vault of heaven
>> and have walked in the depths of the abyss.
> In the waves of the sea, in the whole earth,
>> and in every people and nation I have gotten a
>> possession.
> Among all these I sought a resting place;
>> I sought in whose territory I might lodge.

There are a number of features of this last passage which make it of special interest. (1) Wisdom comes 'from the mouth of the Most High', so that she is virtually a personification of 'the word of God'. (2) While we cannot present the details of the argument here, the passage makes conscious and deliberate use of a variety of themes from the Pentateuch (the first five books of the Old Testament), including the creation accounts in Genesis 1 and 2, and uses language to describe wisdom which is elsewhere reserved for God. This is particularly striking in the phrase 'Alone I have made the circuit of the vault of heaven', which suggests that wisdom was *alone* responsible for creation. Thus the idea of Proverbs 8 has been taken a stage further. Both writers see wisdom as the first of God's creation, both personify her, but only Ben Sira elevates her to a position of sole responsibility. (3) Wisdom is, in a sense, incarnate; she seeks 'a resting place'. In the next verse, Ben Sira goes on to say, 'Then the Creator of all things gave me a commandment, . . . and said, "Make your dwelling in Jacob, and in Israel receive your inheritance".' (4) Despite what has already been said, there is no intention that wisdom should be thought to have supplanted God. He is still the creator of all things (including wisdom), so that in the end we must take Ben Sira's extravagant language about wisdom as being metaphorical.

While I would not wish to exaggerate the influence of this writer, neither should he be dismissed as unimportant. The Book of Ecclesiasticus was undoubtedly popular in the intertestamental period, and was known to the New Testament writers. In particular, I wonder if it is entirely coincidental that in the Prologue to John's Gospel (John 1.1–11) we find an incarnate word present at the very beginning, closely identified with God, and responsible for creation. It may not be unreasonable to suggest that John's metaphorical language is here influenced to some extent by a genuinely Jewish tradition about the nature of wisdom.

The Greek expression used by John in this passage is *logos*, a word which is virtually a technical philosophical term and is only very inadequately translated by our 'word'. Our major source for the background to *logos* is the great Jewish thinker of the first century, Philo of Alexandria. There need not have been any direct influence of Philo on John: it is not necessary to assume that the evangelist had read the works of Philo. It is enough to recognize that the kind of theology and philosophy which Philo represented was very much 'in the air' in the first century, so that a thinker like John would be able to make use of ideas which would be quite familiar to his readers, though less so to those who read him now. Philo had a very 'high' doctrine of the utter and unapproachable transcendence of God. 'For Philo, God is transcendent. Since Scripture presupposes that God exists, his existence is an axiom for Philo. We can know that God exists, but as to our knowing *what* he is, Philo repeatedly assures us that we can never know that.'[3] Nevertheless, we do speak about God; and when we do we are operating in the intelligible world of scripture and reason, where the divine Logos is located. The Logos is thus a kind of intermediary not *reconciling* mankind to God, but *explaining* God to mankind. Philo never works out a systematic presentation of logos-theology; it is doubtful if he had any interest in such systems. But a number of relevant features can be listed: thus, the Logos is the knowable aspect of God; what scripture says about God is ascribed to Logos; the Logos is the supreme 'idea' from which all other archetypal ideas emanate; unlike Platonism, which regarded ideas as eternal and uncreated, Philo saw them as part of God's creation. And although, apart from one indirect reference, Philo does not as a rule refer to incarnation, he does picture the Logos as son of God, with wisdom as mother, and speaks of the Logos as God's first-born or oldest son.

The affinities between this pattern of thinking and the beginning of the Gospel of John are clear. Yet it must be stressed that in no way does Philo present the Logos as equal with God, nor would he have for a moment entertained the notion that the Logos could be identified with a human figure. When John takes these ideas from Philo and Ben Sira and works them into his presentation of Jesus he takes us into a thought-world which is more Jewish than we might at first have imagined, and which, insofar as it *is* Jewish, need not – indeed must not – be interpreted in terms of literal divinity. Once it is transferred to a different context, to the world of Hellenistic thought which eventually became normative for Christianity, other possibilities open out. The point I am concerned to make is that we are likely to see the matter from a position on the other side of that choice. Our 'natural' way of reading the Gospel is to a high degree dependent on the theological assumptions we have inherited, assumptions which result from the transformation of the (Jewish) 'Jesus of history' to the (Christian) 'Christ of the church'. (Readers familiar with the twentieth-century saga of the 'quest for the historical Jesus' and the work of Rudolph Bultmann will recognize here a famous mare's nest! Although the contrast I have employed is undoubtedly naive, it is not, I believe, unmeaningful or unusable. I think we *can* cut through some of the tangle of interpretation to achieve a more realistic portrayal of Jesus the man.)

– 3 –

The various moves we have described in the previous section are quite viable within the characteristic biblical modes of metaphor and myth; it is possible to use them as accounts of reality as long as we recognize their non-literal nature. Thus Paul insists (on the basis of the corrupt state of the whole creation) on the sinfulness of all people and their need for reconciliation with God – a reconciliation which he believes to have been effected by Jesus. In Revelation Jesus occupies a throne and has powers like those of the 'son of man' in Daniel and Enoch. In the Prologue to John's Gospel he is the Logos, the Word present in the beginning at the very moment of creation. We can thus see that the belief in Jesus as a mediator or interpreter of God to humankind is strongly present in the literature of the early church.

Unfortunately the way that these word-pictures have developed has meant that their metaphorical function has been forgotten. We have inherited a system in which philosophical premises about God have been used as the basis of a systematic theology which has left little if any room for myth and metaphor. Our conception of God is now ruled not by the heart but by the head, couched in terms not of wonder and praise but of metaphysical abstraction. The deity is encompassed by a set of absolutes – omniscience, omnipotence, omnipresence, perfect love, total justice – several of which are mutually self-contradictory given the fact of a world in which deserved and undeserved suffering, accidental and premeditated evil exist side by side, and there is precious little justice to be found. It would not be so bad if theologians would take seriously their own claims that no words can adequately express deity; but they proceed to erect on the foundation of these absolutes theological structures which assume them to be axiomatic and logically necessary. The result is the kind of contortionist's act which finds verbal expression in the Council of Chalcedon: the doctrine that Jesus is simultaneously perfect man and perfect God, and that God is at once both three and yet indivisibly one.

Alongside this rigid characterization of God there is an equally strict view of humanity, abstracted from the metaphor of the contaminated nature of the present world order which was popularized in apocalyptic. I mean the doctrine of original sin: somehow, from the very beginning, we have been fallen creatures; and this fallenness is inherent in our very humanity. It is, in a manner of speaking, passed on in the genes. At its Augustinian worst this frightful belief has led Western forms of Christianity (Roman Catholic and reformed alike) into wholesale denigration of sex, and a self-imposed burden of Freudian guilt that makes one wonder about the sanity of the race. I will not linger on the irrationality of taking a legend from Genesis about the origins of the human race to be a serious statement of the biological communicability of sin. Let me simply point out that the Judaeo-Christian understanding of God from Genesis 1 is that he is the sole creator and is therefore ultimately responsible for *everything* in creation – a creation, moreover, that he himself is supposed to have assessed as 'very good'; a creation which included man and woman 'made in his own image'. This point should be well understood today, when so many fundamentalist Americans are going to litigious lengths to have the doctrine (I will not call it a science) of creationism installed in school science curricula. You cannot have it both ways. A God who created a perfect world, and repeatedly commented on how pleased he was with it, cannot be reconciled with the doctrine of the total and irredeemable corruption of that same creation.

The result of linking absolute corruption to absolute love, justice and perfection is, to say the least, mind-boggling. Christianity's early answer was to introduce a wild card, a joker – the god-man – who was able to do what no one else could do, namely to pull himself up by his own bootlaces. This is essentially what 'mediation' seems to be about: the reconciliation of original sin with absolute purity by the instrument of one who had never sinned and was therefore (?) able to pay off the debt of sin to an intransigent yet wholly loving God. This might perhaps work if Jesus were taken to be genuinely and *only* human. But then justice would be affronted (not to mention love), and so the theological importance of Jesus being divine (an idea already endorsed by popular piety and the example of the Graeco–Roman world) was realized. For by identifying Jesus with God the horror of the expiatory sacrifice of an innocent man was averted, and the episode became an edifying example of divine self-sacrifice. Except that the absolute deity cannot be conceived of as having died, and the death of a man who is really a god is of questionable value. You or I might have abandoned the effort at this point, and sought some better understanding of the life, death and resurrection of Jesus. But the early Christian Fathers were made of sterner stuff, and so the delicate (and to most moderns impenetrably obscure) compromise of the God-man and the Trinity was arrived at. My plea is that we are under no obligation to accept these dogmas as truth in defiance of reason and religious instinct – not to mention the evidence of the earliest sources about the human nature of Jesus. To go on repeating them parrot-fashion is pure folly. Only if we can imbue them with some sort of contemporary meaning have we any right at all to say 'this is what *we* believe'. The remainder of this chapter is devoted to an attempt to make sense of Jesus in the light of these preliminary comments.

– 4 –

When the centurion and those who were with him, keeping watch over Jesus, saw the earthquake and what took place, they were filled with awe, and said, 'Truly this was a son of God!'
(Matt. 27.54 [RSV footnote])

That Jesus is of permanent and crucial importance for the whole world is something all Christians take to be a fundamental belief. Yet when we attempt to express that importance in words we find many difficulties in the way. Not the least of these is the very success of Christianity, which has meant that many of the things which appeal most directly to the heart and soul have been shaped by a series of accommodations with popular belief, power structures and secular culture. This is a process which began in Roman times, and can still be seen today in the way that Jesus is reinterpreted in African and Asian terms. In the Western church, for example, teaching on the subject of war has almost always followed rather than formed the attitudes of kings, empires and nation states. And Christmas, one of our most popular and meaningful festivals is replete with beliefs, symbols and practices drawn from the pre- or non-Christian world. This is not necessarily to be regretted. As the church in the world we have a duty to address the world to which we belong in terms that it will understand. At the same time it is the duty of the church's ministers and priests, biblical scholars, historians and theologians to be sensitive both to the inner and deeper meaning of popular forms of faith, and to the spirit of the age, which might well demand other modes for the expression of that faith.

Over the last century popular faith has produced a quite startling range of interpretations of Jesus. We have had, to name only a few, 'gentle Jesus meek and mild'; Jesus the Hero, idol of 'muscular Christianity'; Jesus the revolutionary guerrilla; the hippie saviour of the 'Jesus people'; Jesus as the ethereal, other-worldly object of charismatic adulation; Jesus the Captain of Industry, hero of monetarism, the bomb, WASPs, and the Moral Majority; and Jesus Christ Superstar, the pop re-write of the gospel story. This, though confusing, is very understandable. For what we are witnessing is an increasing desperation in our attempts to make sense, in terms we can understand, of the being and nature of Jesus. Some of these accounts derive from popular piety, a recognition of the attractive-ness of the personality of Jesus on the level of normal human relationships. Indeed for many people it is sufficient to feel that somehow they 'know' Jesus, that the stories about his life and the records of his teaching make him real to us despite the gulf of time and place. There is a genuine and important awareness in this 'naive' response which a number of recent theologians have recognized and explained in such terms as 'theology as story': it is in the significant re-telling of the story that the saving and restoring power of Jesus lies.

Other contemporary accounts, however, are not so innocent. They reflect the interests not of individuals, but of movements, institutions and establishments. They represent a manipulation of Jesus rather than a response to him. We may see this trend in the false portraits of Christ as a revolutionary on the one hand, and as a hyper-respectable moralistic establishment figure on the other. Both are deceitful because they attempt to *use* Jesus for purposes which have nothing to do with anything discernibly part of his own programme. On the analogy of the disciple who betrayed Jesus by trying to manipulate him into declaring the revolution, we might describe this sort of abuse as 'the Judas syndrome'. It *may* be innocently done – Judas may have been an honourable man – but even in that case those who are not honourable, who are far from innocent, are quick to take over and distort the Jesus of history into the false image of their own aspirations. Jesus, of course, is by no means alone in being thus ill-served by his followers. Someone once said, 'All great men have disciples, and it is always Judas who writes their biography!'

None of this is new: earlier ages, too, had their own peculiar ways of describing him. For some, he was a chivalrous knight leading Christian armies to victory; others saw him as a sacrificial lamb; yet again, he played the part of a great judge who simultaneously condemned us and atoned for us. Many of these models were just as manipulative as the more recent ones described above. In the history of the church many very strange things have been done in the name of Christ: the forcible conversion of pagans; the persecution of Jews; the Crusades; the torture, imprisonment and execution of heretics; and the bitter sectarian strife of Northern Ireland, to mention only a few. What *is* new, however, is that the underlying statement which represented the early church's great interpretation of the Master is no longer effective for many people. We cannot now say 'Jesus is divine' without making so many reservations that the statement loses its meaning. The reason for this has little to do with the statement itself, and everything to do with the way we understand language generally. For we are a generation of literalists. Our age is the age of scientific fundamentalism, in which we apply to everything the language which was developed for a very narrow range of experience: the attempt to describe, in quantifiable terms, everything we see or in any way observe. It is the language which says, to parody a little, 'if you can't weigh it, measure it or count it, it isn't there!'

We have largely forgotten the function of metaphor and myth. Whereas these were once respectable means of expressing what could not be said literally, they have been reduced in value until they have become almost terms of abuse. A metaphor is referred to as 'only' a metaphor, and a myth is tantamount to a downright deliberate lie. I know that I cannot singlehandedly put the clock back, but I greatly regret the consequent impoverishment of our theological thinking. From the richness and subtlety of thought which used to characterize theology we are reduced to expecting that expressions such as 'Jesus is divine' should be pseudo-scientific descriptions of observable fact. It can only mean (apparently) that Jesus is 'actually' a god – an interpretation which is palpably false and theologically trivial, on a par with the story in Genesis 3 of the Lord God 'walking in the garden in the cool of the day'; a God, it seems, from whom Adam and Eve can hide, and who has to ask 'Where are you?' All this is fine myth or metaphor; no one imagines that it is history. Yet if we argue that 'Jesus is divine' does not mean that God was born on earth and walked about in Palestine two thousand or so years ago, we are accused of hypocrisy, self-deception and heresy.

— 5 —

What, then, can we say about Jesus? Here are two ways of viewing the matter which can serve as starting points, and which I believe to be faithful to the available historical evidence.

1. There was once a Jew, called Jesus, who was born in Nazareth, where he grew up following his father's trade as a carpenter. About the age of thirty he embarked on a career as a wandering prophet-preacher and healer – a not unknown occupation in that time and place. After a brief and dramatic ministry in which he seems to have offended a good many of the most influential members of his society, he was executed by the Romans by means of crucifixion – their customary method for dealing with non-Roman political offenders. The records show that shortly after his death a number of people reported having seen him again; and within a few years a small but significant group of Jerusalem Jews had acclaimed him as the *Messiah* (or *Christ*) and were actively engaged in spreading this news abroad.

2. In the middle of the first century CE a predominantly non-Jewish movement emerged, taking as its inspiration the life, death and reported resurrection of one Jesus of Nazareth who flourished at some time during the procuratorship of Pontius Pilate. The movement soon spread quite widely throughout the Roman Empire, and began to make claims about Jesus which elevated him from the status of a prophetic human figure in the Jewish tradition to that of a divine being sent to earth by God. After much debate, some of it very violent indeed, this led ultimately to the formulation of the full-blown doctrine of a trinity of persons (Father, Son and Spirit), each held to be fully divine and fully God. It was simultaneously asserted that this in no way denied the oneness and unique being of God. Moreover this same Jesus was defined to be in nature wholly man and wholly God.

These two sketches are not unconnected, though they present essentially different interpretations of Jesus. The New Testament texts, the earliest of which is more than twenty years after the death of Jesus and the latest a hundred, provide evidence for both of them, and reveal something of the process of development.[4] None of them gives a straightforward, realistic biography of Jesus, and none of them approaches anywhere near the elaborate doctrines of the Trinity and the two natures ('wholly man and wholly God') in Jesus which eventually became orthodoxy.

The clear trend of much scholarly work on the Gospels is that the Jewishness of Jesus is hardly in question, though there is some debate about exactly where to place him in the wide spectrum of first-century Judaism. After the discovery of the Dead Sea Scrolls belonging to the ascetic community at Qumran there was considerable enthusiasm for the theory that Jesus was somehow connected, if not with that particular group, at least with the wider movement of *Essenes*. Essene communities were known from antiquity, and described by such writers as the first-century Jewish historian Josephus. They generally lived on the fringes of society, and observed a very strict, almost monkish style of life. It has sometimes been suggested that John the Baptist was of this persuasion. Because of similarities between texts from Qumran and certain of the characteristic writings of the New Testament, there was a superficially plausible case for arguing that Jesus's teachings were Essene in character. However these special features are not restricted to the Qumran materials, and Jesus' behaviour in associating with various suspect groups in society would tend to make it most unlikely that he was closely connected with such an exclusive movement as Essenism. Others have tried to show that Jesus was a Zealot, one of those involved in what can best be described as urban guerrilla warfare against the Romans, and who were implicated in the full-scale revolt in 66 CE. S. G. F. Brandon has argued this case forcefully, but I think unconvincingly, in his book *Jesus and the Zealots*. The evidence is meagre – the incident in the Temple when Jesus knocked over the tradesmen's stalls is quoted with depressing regularity, and with little support from anything else – and it must be stressed that to interpret Jesus as a political revolutionary or a militant liberationist is to do considerable damage to the facts as far as we can determine them.

The only known circles in which to place Jesus (assuming that he was not completely isolated from the community in which he was born) are those of the Pharisees. There have been a great many studies of the Pharisees in recent years, and the superficial and wholly biased account of them given in the Gospels is not now taken as the last word on the subject. It would be well beyond the intended scope of the present work to go into this matter in any detail; but it is important to realize that the Pharisaic movement was by no means monolithic. It contained a wide range of opinion, from very strict to rather liberal, and it was from the ranks of the Pharisees that those great scribes and rabbis came who literally forged what we now recognize as Judaism from the ashes of two devastating defeats in 70 and 134 CE. If I had to recommend just one book on this subject it would be Ellis Rivkin's *A Hidden Revolution*;[5] and not the least reason for recommending it is that it is written from a position of passionate commitment to what the Pharisees stood for, and what they represent as part of a living contemporary faith. All this is a thousand miles away from the distorted Christian view of Judaism as a concoction of dry and dreary legalism. It must be said that Rivkin is somewhat idealistic in his presentation of the Pharisees; but it is perhaps necessary to see the other extreme in order to find the middle.

What this scholarly, rabbinic group stressed particularly was the right interpretation of Torah, the first five books of the Old Testament. They operated with a concept of law as two-fold: Torah on the one hand, and its interpretation and explanation by means of the oral law (the *halakah*) of which they were the creators and guardians. It is widely accepted now that on the evidence of the Gospels Jesus's interests were also centred on Torah (or scripture) and its interpretation. The many disputes recorded by the evangelists, when they are stripped of their gross anti-Jewish bias, indicate that the issues were more often differences of interpretation than differences of principle. Doubtless we ought to place Jesus towards the liberal or 'less observant' end of the Pharisaic spectrum; but he is nonetheless part of that general philosophy rather than an outsider looking in.

The Gospel records are of course not neutral. By the time they came to be written a serious division had taken place between Christians and Jews, and the Christian church was well on the way to becoming part of the Graeco–Roman world in contrast to that of Judaism. Hence the tendency to denigrate the leaders of the Jews – most particularly the Pharisees – and to shift the blame for Jesus's death from the Romans to the Jews. After the first Jewish Revolt in 66–70 CE it was, of course, distinctly not to Christianity's advantage to be identified with Judaism. It is of great significance, then, that the standing of Jesus as a Jew comes across as clearly as it does in the Gospels. His general position is (as we have said) identifiably Pharisaic; and a number of incidents have survived which make it clear that Jesus was indeed a Jew among Jews. The story of the Canaanite woman who came to Jesus to have her daughter healed is instructive. Jesus is reported to have said to her, 'I was sent only to the lost sheep of the house of Israel', and when she persisted in her request, to have gone still further: 'It is not fair to take the children's bread and throw it to the dogs' (Matt. 15.21–28; Mark 7.24–30). However we try to get round it, this story clearly shows us a Jesus who unhesitatingly endorses the idea of the primacy of the

Jews as the 'chosen people'. And when Jesus sends out his disciples (Matt. 10.5–6) he is careful to direct them only to Jewish communities, explicitly forbidding them to preach to Gentiles or Samaritans.

These are, however, just straws in the wind. The prevailing portrayal of Jesus in the Gospels is in the direction of separating him from, successively, his immediate rivals (the Pharisees), his social, cultural and religious context (the Jewish people), and his human nature. We see this worked out in several ways:

(a) The polemic against the Pharisees in the Synoptic Gospels (so-called because they have in common a considerable body of material, and are dependent on each other. Mark is probably the earliest – c. 70 CE – and the other two, while adding material of their own, make extensive use of him). Matthew particularly seems to intend to draw as sharp a contrast as possible between Jesus and his co-religionists. The bitterness of some of this material – especially Matthew 23 – suggests that there is almost a love-hate relationship between the followers of Jesus and the followers of the Pharisees. It is tempting to conclude that they were in fact rather close to each other, and that the dispute was of the nature of a family quarrel. Family feuds are, of course, always the most bitter.

(b) In John's Gospel the attack on Jesus's enemies is generalized to 'the Jews', as if to say that Jesus himself was not a Jew. And the accounts of the trial and death of Jesus similarly allocate blame to all sections of the Jewish community, so that a non-Jewish reader, sensing the 'us-them' nature of the presentation, almost unconsciously picks up an anti-Jewish polemic from them. Whatever the rights and wrongs of the matter, and wherever the responsibility ultimately lies, it is a gross over-simplification to argue (as many do): 'Jesus was the Messiah; the Jews had him executed; therefore the Jews have rejected their long-awaited Messiah.'

(c) The ultimate stage in the Christian appropriation of Jesus was reached in the deification of the Christ. There is no doubt that the New Testament knows of Jesus as 'son of God' and 'Lord' (a term closely associated with the personal name of God, Yahweh, in the Old Testament); and the prologue to John's Gospel refers to him as the 'Logos', a term (as we have seen already) which expressed a particularly close relationship to the deity. To what extent these terms *as used in the New Testament* have moved from Jewish metaphor to pagan literalism is a matter of debate. What is clear is that within thirty to forty years of Jesus' death a movement towards the deification of the man was well under way.

Out of all this I want to make one simple point: the New Testament evidence is of a radical conflict in interpretation. That

Jesus was a Jew of the Pharisaic school, with many of the commonly held attitudes of good but not excessively zealous Jews, seems reasonably well established. That the church, by the manner of its telling of the life and death and resurrection of Jesus, effectively separated him from that milieu and presented him much more as a divine figure, seems equally certain. There is thus at the very heart of the gospel a dilemma.

We began this section by offering two sketches towards an understanding of Jesus. On the whole, the second became the more persuasive interpretation, because it suited much better the Greek branch of the church which soon dominated. Yet the first did not entirely disappear. For a considerable period there continued to be Jewish Christians (the Epistle of James may have originated in that sort of milieu), and several New Testament passages bear witness to a struggle between those who saw Christianity as firmly within the community of Judaism, and those who desired to split it off from everything Jewish. Jesus himself, as a devout and faithful Jew, could not personally have claimed to be divine; nor could he have accepted that claim made of him by anyone else. Acts 14.8–18 is instructive here: when Paul and Barnabas were hailed as gods by the crowd in Lystra they were greatly agitated, and went to considerable lengths to disabuse the people of their blasphemous notion. *That* is an authentic Jewish response. Not only was it psychologically and religiously impossible for Jesus to have made such a claim, it is historically false to say that he did. For he was *not* executed for blasphemy. He was executed, by the Romans, for offences against the state. The Jews at that time had the power of capital punishment in purely religious matters; and had Jesus been guilty of the blasphemy of claiming to be God they would have dealt with him swiftly, and with popular consent! (It was not, by the way, blasphemy in Jewish eyes to claim to be the Messiah.) When later generations passed the sentence of 'divinity' on Jesus, they made a judgment which was essentially non-Jewish, motivated by an understanding of the relationship between the divine and the human which was by no means strange to the gentile world. Thus we have a rather paradoxical consequence: Jesus the Jew was deemed by Gentiles to be that which he could not conceivably have claimed to be – a god incarnate. And as a result of that judgment, his own people were excluded from following the one whom some of them at least had already recognized as the Messiah.

Nothing we have said denies, or is intended to deny, the historical fact that this radical sect of first-century Judaism, far from disappearing as one might have expected, survived and matured into a religion of remarkable vitality and tenacity. In all probability, had it remained within the confines of Judaism it would never have reached such a wide community. The key to this phenomenon is, as we have already indicated, the introduction and central development of what was essentially an alien doctrine: the divine nature of the man Jesus and his role as intermediary between God and man. We have seen that there is a tradition in apocalyptic literature which speaks of a kind of intermediary; but there he is an angelic rather than a human figure. The human agent of apocalyptic, even when he is (as in the case of Enoch) ecstatically borne into the presence of God, remains a bearer of revelation, not mediation. It is thus more appropriate to look to Graeco-Roman thought forms for this innovation – an innovation which, when combined with the tremendous *moral* force of Judaism, proved strongly attractive to the non-Jewish world.

Such a radical transformation does not, of course, come entirely out of the blue. Some catalyst or cause is to be expected, and we need surely look no further than the resurrection to find an adequate spiritual and psychological impetus for the later theological rationale. The centrality of the death and resurrection of Jesus in the thinking of the early church is undoubted. It is generally accepted that the passion and resurrection narratives belong to the very earliest strata of the gospel tradition, an observation further supported by the extent to which Paul stresses the importance of the resurrection. We have, in the passion narratives, eloquent testimony to the 'event' which gave birth to the church. But having said this, it must be emphasized that these are matters of interpretation, explanation, and of coming to terms with a traumatic experience. The records show clearly that by the time they came to be written down they had been greatly influenced by the theology of the early church. And that theology had developed along the lines of closely linking resurrection with a divine nature. This development was not inherent in the idea of resurrection. Indeed, the doctrine of the resurrection of the individual and the survival of death was, in both Judaism and Christianity, applied to all human beings – not just those in possession of a 'divine nature'. But because of the growing belief (perhaps influenced by the Greek and Roman practice of recognizing great kings as gods) that Jesus was not just metaphorically, but *literally* the Son of God, his resurrection came to be seen as proof of his divine status. The trouble with this connection is that, just as the performance of a miracle is convincing only to those who are already convinced, so the meaning of the resurrection is (I believe) trivialized if it is reduced to a legalistic argument in defence of the unprovable – that Jesus was God incarnate.

In view of all this it would be fair to ask, 'Can we still say, "I believe in Jesus?"' My emphatic answer would be 'Yes: I for one am an enthusiastic believer in Jesus!' But it is the Jesus who walked this earth, who lived and died and rose to life in Palestine, in whom I believe. I accept the inspiration of scripture and its status as a norm of Christian belief. But I do not accord similar status to councils and creeds, and find it hard to understand why a church which claims to be dependent on scripture as its authority should need to resort to the doctrinal formulations of Chalcedon (451 CE) or of Westminster (1646 CE) and accord them the status of near-absolute truth. Both of these expressions of belief are necessarily limited by time and place, and our duty is surely to seek for our own day the meaning of the one in whom we believe, examining the sources with as much skill as we can muster. And in the end the truth we seek, the living truth, will be expressed in mythic rather than scientific terms. Peter Redgrove has said that 'poetry is the natural mode of the mind', and truths of a poetic nature can never be reduced to just one set of formal propositions. That would be tantamount to saying that myth or metaphor could be better expressed in the language of logic or mathematics – a plainly absurd conclusion.

Who then is this Jesus whom we call Messiah? Historically, a man who heard God's call and obeyed; who followed that obedience through to the ultimate point – and beyond; who matched, as few have ever done, his teaching with his deeds. To the eye of faith he signifies hope for humanity, the embodiment of love. His being chosen by God, his faithfulness to that call, and his fulfilment (through suffering, death, and resurrection) of the ministry of the Messiah – all these give us hope in the final victory of love. The power and importance of love in this strong sense is often underestimated. It is something other than passion, though lovers must be passionate. It has nothing to do with romance, and everything to do with commitment. It is not a question of liking, but it demands caring of a costly and self-denying character. It is the meaning of life and the mastery of death. One of the few theologians who gave this love systematic content and who stressed it as the essential meaning of the cross, a man called Abelard, was rejected by the church as a heretic, and his teaching proscribed. The founder of that same church was crucified for his love.

As I look around at a world in which every new day seems to bring new cause for despair; in which women and children lose their lives in the name of 'patriotism', 'sovereignty' and (most blasphemously of all) 'freedom'; in which the poor starve and go naked in order that proper tribute may be paid to the new gods Cruise, Pershing and Trident – as I look at this world only one thing gives me hope: the unaccountable power and persistence of love, the proof that the God who made us has not abandoned us.

Jesus is, in the end, God's representative, who both teaches us the nature of love and lives out his own teaching. He who said, 'Greater love has no man than this, that a man lay down his life for his friends', is the same man whose love took him to death. He is not the only human being to have done this; but that sacrifice, whenever it is offered, is not to be despised. For there are few indeed who know the nature of love, fewer still who live it, and one or two only who die for it. So when I look at the cross, and remember that there a fellow human being made the ultimate sacrifice that love can make, I know that it was for me, and people like me, that it was done. And when I contemplate the mystery of the resurrection I am persuaded not by the notion that a god should have conquered death (in itself an unremarkable thing), but by the wonder that human life, through love, is stronger than death. In Jesus the Messiah, the chosen and anointed servant of God, in his teaching, his living, his dying and his coming to life, I see the reality of that love which is of God, and belief becomes possible.

6

Creeds for Christians

Having spent some time discussing what we might mean by some of the things we commonly say about Jesus, we can now attempt to describe the kind of statements Christians could be expected to make if asked to define their beliefs. The arguments developed in Chapter 5 will prepare us for a certain amount of disagreement, and a considerable degree of obscurity (not all of it attributable to the present writer's method of presentation!). On the one hand, the very existence of creeds, of detailed statements of belief, is evidence for lack of consensus: the ancient creeds were almost without exception drawn up in response to disputes within the church which required clarification – or, more often, an authoritative decision. Obscurity, on the other hand, is a function of two things: the passage of time, which makes it exceptionally difficult for us to recover the original sense and nuance of the language used; and a shift in theological emphasis which means that many issues which were vital and controversial in the early church are now of no concern to us. How many Christians in Western churches are today even peripherally aware that the church was once torn asunder by a bitter dispute as to whether the Holy Spirit proceeded from the Father *and* the Son, or only from the Father? How many would be able to say which side of the argument was supported by the Western church? Does it matter? No doubt it does for those who find themselves engaged in theological debate with scholars of the Orthodox churches; but it would have to be admitted that this somewhat recondite possibility is hardly a major factor on the contemporary scene. Yet the Nicene Creed, which is used very regularly in worship in the Western tradition, makes a particular point of referring to this controversy in its article on the Holy Ghost.

The obvious place to begin an attempt at isolating the 'essentials of the faith' is with the creeds. Plainly a comprehensive treatment of creeds is out of the question – there are far too many of them. But a certain methodology suggests itself, which will I hope also find favour with the reader. There are two ancient creeds of high standing in the church at large which are very widely used. These are the Apostles' Creed and the Nicene Creed. Both are readily accessible in a number of set liturgies and hymnals – in the *Church Hymnary* (Third Edition), for example, they can be found at numbers 546 and 558 respectively – so I will not reproduce them here. I propose to consider them as evidence for the fundamental shape of Christian belief at a time when theological thinking was well advanced in the early church, but before the great (and I believe restrictive) codifications of Chalcedon and after. Along with these two I will allow my own denominational background to influence a further selection: the Scots Confession of 1560; the Westminster Confession (composed in 1646 and approved by the General Assembly of the Church of Scotland in 1647); and the First Article Declaratory of the uniting Church of Scotland, 1929.[1] The last of these is not strictly a creed, being held as a summary of the faith of the church. The distinction is perhaps an over-fine one, and since it has recently been proposed that it be given the official status of a definition of the fundamentals of the faith,[2] it will serve as possibly the most up-to-date authoritative statement available in the Church of Scotland.

The selection of documents relating to one particular denomination is not as restrictive or sectarian as at first appears. The comparisons to be made are intended to show (a) to what extent there is agreement even within one denomination, (b) how far the particular interests of that specific tradition have distanced it from the early creeds, and (c) (hopefully!) wherein lies the real core of Christian belief. The end result, far from endorsing those things which are peculiar to the Church of Scotland, or the Reformed traditions in general, will be much more likely to reveal just how peripheral are many issues deemed from within the tradition to be central. This conclusion is not, of course, restricted to Presbyterianism. We could substitute Anglicanism, Roman Catholicism, or Orthodoxy and arrive at a very similar destination. None of this is intended to minimize the fruitful and necessary character of the different forms in which Christianity is now manifest. What we are saying is simply the very obvious: what is of the essence of 'Christianity' cannot be the sole prerogative of only one denomination or tradition. Not all Christians are Presbyterian, despite the

Church of Scotland's occasional delusions of grandeur! There is an inevitably minimalist aspect to this endeavour which may well discredit it in many eyes. Most Christians are, after all, not adherents of some generalized or idealized abstraction of 'the faith', but members of specific churches; and very often what is dearest to us is not the core of the universal faith, but the time- and place-conditioned features of 'our own' church. Nevertheless, if there is to be any hope for dialogue, we must reach the stage of seeing that these cherished particularities are the very things that don't matter. Whether or not we baptize infants; whether there are two sacraments or seven or none at all; whether we have bishops or presbyters, archdeacons or patriarchs, ministers or priests; all of these (and a hundred thousand others) constitute things that can never be of the *esse* of the Christian church. Whether any of them are of the *bene esse*[3] is a question that, happily, we need not pursue here.

— 2 —

The single most obvious comment to make on the creeds we have chosen is that they all operate within the broad framework of God–Jesus–Holy Spirit. The obviously trinitarian nature of this pattern cannot be denied. But it is rather interesting that neither of the ancient creeds makes explicit reference to the Trinity, or to God's being 'three in one', whereas each of the Scottish post-Reformation documents is careful to spell it out in so many words:

One in substance and yet distinct in three persons.
(Scots Confession)

In the unity of the Godhead there be three persons, of one substance, power, and eternity.   (Westminster Confession)

Worshipping one God . . . in the Trinity of the Father, the Son, and the Holy Ghost, the same in substance, equal in power and glory.   (Articles Declaratory)

Along with this explicit emphasis, these three introduce variations on the basic framework corresponding to the dominating concerns of their composers. The preface to the Scots Confession makes plain the Reformers' consciousness of being primarily dependent on scripture. This is reflected in the articles (II–V) which come between the first article, on God, and those dealing with Jesus; for they deal in broad outline with the 'history' of God's dealing with mankind from creation to the coming of Jesus, as set out in the narrative and historical books of the Old Testament (Genesis – Kings). Despite its inevitably sexist language, and an understandable lack of moderation in the way it represents the Roman Catholic persuasion, the Scots Confession is arguably the most attractive (perhaps because least scholastically Calvinist) of the reformed creeds. There is, in its presentation, something of a foreshadowing of the 'Salvation History' school of biblical theology which, in the 1940s and 50s, sought to interpret the Bible as the record of God's dealings in history with his people, always working towards the final realization in Jesus of his great plan of salvation.

The Westminster Confession departs most radically from the pattern of the Apostles' and the Nicene Creeds. It begins not with God but with a lengthy exposition of the doctrine of the authority, inspiration and infallibility of scripture. And immediately after the article concerning God there is an account of that extreme form of Calvinist doctrine known as 'double predestination':

> By the decree of God, for the manifestation of His glory, some men and angels are predestined unto everlasting life; and others foreordained to everlasting death.   (Chapter III, section III)

Thereafter the Confession proceeds, rather like the Scots Confession, from Creation, Providence and Fall through the Covenant of the Old Testament, to the incarnation of Christ. But where the older document was couched almost in narrative form, we now find a much more developed theology, with only the most perfunctory references to the Old Testament scriptures. One further difference may be mentioned at this point. Unlike all the other examples we are considering, the Westminster Confession does not devote any article specifically to the Holy Spirit. This is not to suggest that the third member of the Trinity is omitted – far from it – but the Spirit always appears (apart from a purely formal notification in Chapter II, section III) in a functional capacity, not as a person to be 'believed in'. A similar deficiency is discernible when the First Article Declaratory refers to 'trusting in the promised renewal and guidance of the Holy Spirit'.

The latter, allowing for this reservation, follows the standard pattern, but prefaces it with an ecclesiological declaration when it asserts: 'The Church of Scotland is part of the Holy Catholic or Universal Church.' Not too much need be made of this, since it stands within the context of documents defining the status and character of the uniting church; and in fact down to the clause 'the gift of Eternal Life' it matches the Apostles' Creed fairly closely. The churchly interest is, however, intruded into the passage dealing with Jesus, where the clause 'owning obedience to Him as the Head over all things to His Church' sounds suspiciously like a piece of Presbyterian polemic against the suggestion that any human figure could be given the status of 'Head of the Church'.

A preliminary summary will be helpful at this stage:

1. We have seen that all the creeds under examination are founded on the threefold pattern of God/Jesus/Holy Spirit.

2. Neither of the ancient creeds mentions trinity explicitly; all of the post-Reformation ones do.

3. Each of the confessions from the reformed church in Scotland exhibits some bias which results from its particular context; in each case this bias interrupts the underlying framework to some extent, though without wholly distorting it.

4. There is a tendency (I would not wish to put it more strongly) to effectively reduce the status of the third person of the Trinity, the Spirit, to that of a means towards the achievement of certain desirable spiritual ends rather than an end in itself, deserving of belief and worship like the Father and the Son. Whether this phenomenon is a cause or an effect of the notorious legalism of Scottish Presbyterianism I leave to the reader to decide!

The two great historical confessions which are linked with the Scottish Church discuss the order of the church and its institutions in some detail, as might be expected; and we have already noted that the First Article Declaratory, within its more limited compass, also emphasizes the church. In its concluding lines it further defines it allegiance to a particular form of church polity as represented by the Scottish Reformation. All of this is perfectly reasonable, and falls within the scope of that which defines the church as a particular denomination. None of it should be taken as fundamental to faith or to any proposed definition of Christianity. There are, though, three doctrines which are strongly insisted upon in these documents, and which are quite lacking from the Apostles' and Nicene Creeds. They are:

A. The supreme authority of scripture;
B. The doctrine of original sin;
C. The doctrine of election and predestination.

While none of these is by itself unique to presbyterianism, the combination of them together with the emphasis placed on them (particularly in the Westminster Confession) is a fair indication of the Calvinist origins of this branch of the church. *It is reasonable therefore to discount them as possible candidates for our set of fundamental beliefs.* Not one of them is universally accepted in the church at large; indeed they are all the subject of controversy even within presbyterianism.

What I wish to claim here is that the threefold framework is common to all five confessions or creeds, and that where the reformed statements depart from or alter this framework they do so under the influence of clearly sectarian requirements which, however valuable they may be for defining the character of a particular branch of the church, can have no place in the fundamental definition of Christian faith. In the next section we will turn to the two ancient creeds and try to ascertain some basic guidelines.

— 3 —

There can be no doubt that any creed which claimed to describe Christianity would have to say something about Jesus, without whom there would *be* no such faith. Equally certainly there would have to be an account of what was understood by 'God'; for no one has ever denied that Christianity is a deistic religion. Its Jewish roots would in any case ensure that this be a primary concern, given the enormous stress placed by Judaism on the supremacy of the one God. The clearest example is that passage from Deuteronomy 6.4–5 (known as the *shema* from the first word of its Hebrew text) which is in a very real sense the Jewish credo *par excellence*:

> Hear, O Israel: Yahweh is our God; Yahweh is One; and you shall love Yahweh your God with all your heart, and with all your soul, and with all your might.

And it is *almost* certain that a place would have to be found for the Holy Spirit, though we have already seen that by the time of the Nicene Creed there is serious controversy regarding the correct expression of this point, while the post-Reformation confessions further depart from a simple principle of 'three persons'.

The order and number of these fundamental beliefs is not unimportant. The primacy of God, for example, is well-established. Even where later documents introduce a preliminary clause, such as the authority of scripture in the Westminster Confession, the nature and person of God is still the first concern in describing the Trinity. While this may seem straightforward, it has to be insisted upon, for there have been Christian theologies which have begun with Jesus on the grounds that he is our only revealed source of knowledge of God. Such 'Christocentric' presentations were popular a few years ago, and their emotional impact can still be seen in that form of piety often found amongst charismatics in which prayers and worship are addressed almost exclusively to Jesus. Some popular movements of the sixties like the 'Jesus People' similarly focussed on Jesus as if he was their God. Now whatever Christian orthodoxy may claim about the divine nature of Jesus, it has never sought thereby to *substitute* him for God. Any move in this direction would have to be recognized as radically new, whatever its merits, and might conceivably be one of the findings of a dialogical rethinking of the Christian position. Though even as I write the words 'radically new' I am reminded by the Preacher's wise dictum, 'There is nothing new under the sun', that in the early years of the church Marcion proposed something similar when he rejected Yahweh, the God of the Old Testament, as an evil, alien deity who had been replaced by the new revelation in Jesus – seen as a direct representative of the true God who transcended the evil and fallen world in which Yahweh held sway. Whatever the value, then, of a christocentric approach it could scarcely be one of the fundamental presuppositions of orthodox Christianity. On the other hand, something as seemingly accidental as the number of leading persons in the creed does appear to be essential. Leaving aside the question of their relationship and relative significance, the 'three-ness' of God has been a characteristic Christian expression from very early times, as we can see from certain additions to the New Testament text like the primitive baptismal formula in Matthew 28.19 which may represent the practice of the Syrian church around the end of the first century. And although it would be difficult to derive a coherent *doctrine* of 'the Trinity' from the New Testament (and impossible from the Old), the first-century church was obviously at home with the kind of language about 'God', 'Jesus Christ' and the 'Spirit' which held within it the seeds of later speculative theology.

We have spoken, in Chapter 5,[4] of the antecedents of the account of Jesus which came to be dominant in the early church, and we have emphasized the way that certain ideas characteristic of Jewish thinking in the intertestamental period had been reshaped under the influence of Hellenistic philosophy. There is no doubt that, well short of deification, there is much in the Christian Jesus which is (at least in origin) indebted to Jewish concepts of that time. Similarly, we can trace a significant Hebrew background for the third 'person' of the later Trinity. The Spirit was well-established in Jewish thought and religious language, which was perfectly at home with the concept of the spirit (*rûah*) of God and its rôle as an empowering force. It moves over the face of the primeval waters at creation (Gen. 1.2). Numbers 11 describes how the spirit which is in Moses can be passed on to the seventy elders appointed to assist him. In Numbers 27.18 Joshua is chosen to succeed Moses because he is 'a man in whom is the spirit'. Several of the charismatic leaders in Judges are compelled by the Spirit of Yahweh (Othniel, 3.10; Gideon, 6.34; Jephthah, 11.29; Samson, 13.25; 14.6, 19; 15.4). That same spirit is associated with the messiah in Isaiah 11.2, and with God as creator in 40.13. It is the spirit which inspires Ezekiel (e.g. 2.2; 3.14; 11.5 etc.) and is attributed to Isaiah in an editorial gloss (59.21). The famous passage quoted by Jesus in his sermon in the synagogue at Nazareth begins, 'The Spirit of the Lord God is upon me' (Isa. 61.1). In Micah 3.8 the prophet identifies the Spirit of the Lord with the power of prophecy which fills him.

In the light of these and many other examples it is clear that Christian language about the Spirit is well rooted in the Jewish background, and can be contained in a strictly monotheistic framework. This is because all such language is defined and limited by the fundamental axiom: God is one. Therefore whatever form of words we use to describe God or his activity in the world, it can never be read in such a way as to deny that essential belief. The Spirit in the Old Testament was not taken to be a divine personage alongside God; it was simply one of the *modes* of God's activity. Similarly Wisdom, the Word, and the Glory of God are personified, but not understood to be deified. They are ways of understanding God which belong to the sphere of metaphor or analogy, and which are appropriate in different contexts. Even if later Christianity chose to travel the Trinitarian route (in the Chalcedonian sense), it has no grounds for building that retrospectively into the Old Testament. I have, of course, further argued that there was no compelling reason even within a Christian understanding of Jesus to adopt this paradigm. It is a hypothesis we do not really need, unless *for some reason extrinsic to the Jewish origins of the faith* we feel compelled to make rigorous philosophical sense of the different modes of understanding which constitute our verbal 'imagery' of God as Father, Son and Spirit.

The conclusion so far is that the following represent fundamental elements of any definition of the Christian faith:

1. The oneness of God.
2. The central importance of Jesus.
3. The Spirit as an expression of God's activity.
4. An assertion of the 'three-ness' of our awareness of God.

These brief, somewhat cryptic statements do not end the matter. On the one hand they can be further spelled out, and on the other, additional statements may be made which give more of the characteristic 'colour' of Christianity. We will proceed now to give a more detailed account.

$$- 4 -$$

1. *Of God*

God is described as father, and is held to be the creator of all that is. These attributes, together with his uniqueness and oneness, are essential features of most Christian creeds.

There is a genuine difficulty with talk about God. For if we take seriously the transcendence of the deity, we face the problem that it is in principle impossible to say anything at all about 'him'. (Including any implication of maleness or gender: the growing controversy in certain church circles about the motherhood of God and the female principle in deity is right to challenge the male language of the patriarchal God, but surely wrong if it seeks to arrange a direct substitution of female for male. No doubt some of the things we wish to say about the creator will be 'feminine', just as some will be 'masculine'; and certainly the bias has too often and for too long been towards the latter. But the problem is not solved by addressing God as 'she', unless of course that language is designed not so much to describe God as to shock complacent male theologians out of their self-satisfied male-hierarchical conventions.) If, with Philo, we take the existence of God to be axiomatic, to be a fundamental premise of belief, it may be that we would be best to stop speculating at that point. However, even Philo had to say more, although he did so by speaking (at great length) of an intermediate realm in which the unknowable God had made himself/herself/itself in some degree accessible to humanity. And it is undoubtedly a central principle of all religions that *some* form of revelation has taken place. Since all of these are of necessity mediated through human beings, they are equally necessarily analogical, allegorical, metaphorical, mythical: in short, they are bound by all the usual limitations of human language and human thought.

A particular feature of Christian theology, with its considerable indebtedness to Greek philosophy, has been a constant striving after a system of theology which would be logically consistent and coherent. At the same time, under the influence of neo-Platonism, great importance was placed on the use of absolute categories to describe God. The justice, love, power, knowledge, presence of the deity had to have in addition the quality of perfection. Two fundamental problems derive from this approach. First, there is an in-built logical incoherence to the combination of absolute love, absolute justice and absolute power. A God of perfect power cannot coexist with any real force of evil: all that happens in creation must be according to God's will. A God of perfect justice cannot find guilty those whose sin is part of that deity's own creation. A God of perfect love cannot permit the ultimate damnation of any creature: to do so would be an affront to love and justice, and proof of the limitations of God's power. The second problem (which to some extent explains the first) is that the language of absolutes is inherently beyond the scope of the human mind. We can only use contingent and imperfect analogies to present the supposed absolutes which define the deity, and so the endeavour is damagingly flawed from the very beginning. If all this were just a matter of speculative theology it might be an innocent enough diversion; but it sadly has practical implications which we cannot afford to ignore. The use of the language of absolutes to describe God leads too easily to the assumption that such language has the quality of absolute truth – a self-deception which opens the door wide to intolerance, bigotry and narrow-minded exclusivism. The theology of dialogue, therefore, must recognize that our attempts to present the nature of God are an exercise not in philosophical truth but in dialogue. Far better to be modest in our claims to know God; and if that modesty drives us to complete silence (as has been the case for some), perhaps the silence of humility is a more accurate picture of the deity than the ravings of the religious zealots whose message too often comes across as not love, but 'hate your neighbour'. All of this leads me to feel that lists of the qualities of God, such as that found at the beginning of the second chapter of the Westminster Confession, should be avoided. But in order to show what we thereby lose, let me reproduce that list here:

There is but one only, living, and true God, who is infinite in being and perfection, a most pure spirit, invisible, without body, parts, or passions; immutable, immense, eternal, incomprehensible, almighty, most wise, most holy, most free, most absolute; working all things according to the counsel of His own immutable and most righteous will, for His own glory; most loving, gracious, merciful, long-suffering, abundant in goodness and truth, forgiving iniquity, transgression, and sin; the rewarder of them that diligently seek Him; and withal, most just, and terrible in His judgments, hating all sin, and who will by no means clear the guilty.

Given that any language we use about God will inevitably be anthropomorphic, my personal inclination is to make enthusiastic use of this limitation. I find, for example, that I have a natural empathy for those passages where the Old Testament presents God almost as one of the characters in the story. I am attracted by the God who walks in the Garden of Eden in the cool of the day. I am very much drawn to the deity who is willing to debate with Abraham virtually as an equal over the matter of how to deal with Sodom (Gen. 18.16–33). If God loves and cares for the created world and all its various forms (as I believe is the case) then I have no psychological difficulty making a naive identification of that divine caring in the kind of terms implied by these biblical instances. To argue, quarrel or engage in dialogue with God seems to me to be a reasonable thing to do. But only as long as we do not make the mistake of confusing these helpful conventions with any more permanent or profound statement about the nature of God. And, more importantly, so long as we do not claim that what proves useful for some must be prescriptive for all. I suspect that all we can say in the hope of winning general agreement is, 'God is'. Beyond that we are forced to make the best we can of language with all its limitations to say meaningful things about that which is beyond meaning, to draw helpful comparisons to describe the incomparable, and to make real and immediate that which is the transcendent author of our reality. It may seem like a vain endeavour, yet it is one to which the religious mind is constantly driven, and from which men and women of faith draw real inspiration.

I take it to be generally held by all branches of the Christian church that God is the creator, the *fons et origo*, of the whole sensible and intelligible universe, and that this belief entails both the oneness and the uniqueness of the deity. Further, it seems to be generally accepted that God retains an interest in what has been thus created, an interest which is usually described (in English at any rate) by the word 'love'. The meaning of that word is perhaps best determined by what we conceive the rôle of Jesus to be; the conventional way to express God's involvement in this process is to refer to the deity as 'father', a description of God found in most creeds. We may perhaps retain this title if we understand it not as an attribute but as a means of specifying a relationship (and a metaphorical means at that). It should therefore not be interpreted from the emotional aspect of family life, and does not depend on how 'good' or 'bad' any particular human father may be. There are undoubtedly places in scripture where this metaphor is used, Psalm 103.13 being perhaps the most familiar ('As a father pities his children, so the Lord pities those who fear him.'). But it is well to remember that God is also spoken of in maternal terms in Hosea 11.1–4:

> When Israel was a child, I loved him,
>   and out of Egypt I called my son.
> The more I called them,
>   the more they went from me;
> they kept sacrificing to the Baals,
>   and burning incense to idols.
> Yet it was I who taught Ephraim to walk,
>   I took them up in my arms;
>   but they did not know that I healed them.
> I led them with cords of compassion,
>   and with the bands of love,
> and I became to them as one
>   who eases the yoke on their jaws,
>   and I bent down to them and fed them.

In view of the inevitably controversial associations which both of these terms invoke, it may be that we should dispense with them altogether and look for something more neutral. Perhaps 'God the begetter and creator', if not too archaic, would serve.

– 5 –

2. *Of Jesus*

(a) Jesus is God's Son, and our Lord.

(b) He is a mediator between God and humankind.

(c) His human birth, life and death are not in question, and can be specifically located in history.

(d) It is claimed that he rose from the dead, is now with God, and will be reponsible for carrying out the final judgment at the end of time.

In Chapter 5 I discussed at some length the possibility of an interpretation of the sonship of Jesus which does not assume divinity. Such an approach is not unprecedented in Christian discussion and need not be ruled out automatically, as the controversy surrounding the elevation of David Jenkins to the See of Durham in 1984 makes clear. Vociferous opposition was raised to his consecration on the grounds that he had expressed doubts about the divinity of Jesus. Yet the Archbishop of York – a far from radical figure – defended his appointment, and duly consecrated Jenkins at York Minster on 6 July. That there was a disastrous fire (apparently caused by lightning) in the Minster very soon afterwards was no doubt a coincidence; but some of the more extreme evangelicals were unable to resist the temptation to see the hand of God at work in swift, if somewhat misplaced retribution!

The portrayal of Jesus as mediator received some attention in our discussion of Philo and the Logos in Chapter 5, where it was emphasized that mediation is to be understood in an explanatory rather than a reconciliatory mode. At this point something should be said about the belief that Jesus was the Messiah – a claim strangely missing from both the Apostles' and the Nicene Creeds, being retained only in the use of the title 'Christ'. It does receive a more deliberate treatment in the Scots Confession (chapters V, VI, VII) and in the Westminster Confession (VII.V), though it is not developed in any way, and is largely subsumed under the title 'Christ'. While the two titles are theoretically the same, *christ* being Greek for the Hebrew *messiah*, I suspect that the former gains greater currency precisely because it is distanced from any prior Jewish conceptions, and more readily permits the kind of radical redefinition which the church had to carry out in order to justify the claim that Jesus was the fulfilment of the expectations of the Jews based on their sacred scriptures. For the Jesus defined by the Nicene Creed as 'God of God, Light of Light, Very God of Very God, begotten, not made, being of one substance with the Father' is a very different figure from the Messiah awaited by Jews of the first century CE.

The idea of a messiah who would be God's agent in bringing about the consummation of history, and who would reign over the perfect kingdom of God, was current in certain Jewish circles between 100 BCE and 100 CE. The Psalms of Solomon, dating from the mid-first century BCE, contain a long passage giving a picture of the Davidic messiah.[5] He 'is a human being, a member of the family of David. He is a latter-day fulfilment of God's ancient promise that the sons of David would rule over Israel *in perpetuum*. . . . The author alludes to the biblical oracles, especially Psalm 2.9 and Isaiah 11.2–5. Although the messianic king will be a human being, the author attributes to him certain semi-divine characteristics. . . . He is the presence of wisdom, strength, and righteousness . . . and is pure from sin'.[6] His function is to gather together the nations of the earth, to judge them, and to establish the ideal kingdom of God, with himself as the righteous king in Jerusalem. Other pre-Christian sources of messianic material are found amongst the Qumran documents; and though these seem to envisage a division of responsibilities between two messiahs, the main features are not unlike those found in the Psalms of Solomon. The connections with certain familiar prophetic passages in the Old Testament are clear enough; and from Christian descriptions of the last days in Revelation we know that the same hopes were cherished in first-century church circles. But there is a crucial difference. The Jewish messiah, insofar as the concept remains a live one, is still awaited; the Christian one has been – and gone – and apparently the prophecies remain unfulfilled.

It is generally true that messianism is not a major part of most modern Judaism (a fact that often surprises Christians, who are used to language which understands the Hebrew scriptures as primarily, if not exclusively, concerned with the coming of the Messiah). There is a rather fine description of the messianic hope from a modern Jewish perspective in Isidore Epstein's *Judaism*.[7] I make no apology for repeating it in full here:

> The Kingdom of God in the scheme of Judaism will be ushered in by the Messiah. The Messiah will be the central dominating figure of an age which will witness the reign of righteousness on earth, a righteousness which will bring universal peace and plenty, plenty of the things necessary for a righteous life, without taking away the need for sacrifice on behalf of ever-widening and growing ideals. But the Messiah in Jewish teaching is not a supernatural being, nor a divine being, having a share in the forgiveness of sin; much less is he to be confused with God. At the highest the Messiah is but a mortal leader who will be instrumental in fully rehabilitating Israel in its ancient homeland, and through a restored Israel bring about the moral and spiritual regeneration of the whole of humanity, making all mankind fit citizens of the Kingdom. Then shall the reign of the Lord be universal. In the words of the prophet 'The Lord shall be King over all the earth, in that day shall the Lord be one and His name one' (Zech. 14.9); and in this universality [sic] a true religion, professed by all men and realized in their lives in all their relations to God and their fellow-men, shall divine purpose on earth find its fulfilment.

The Kingdom of God in its Messianic setting and earthly fulfilment is but preparatory to the consummation of the Kingdom in the supra-historical world to come, a world which in rabbinic parlance 'No ear hath heard, nor eye hath seen' (cf. Isa. 64.3[4]). With this supra-historical and supernatural order of things are associated the doctrines of the resurrection of the dead and the universal Day of Judgment, when the end of all the ways of God will be made known, and the fullest consummation of His purpose shall be accomplished.

The problem Christianity had to face right at the beginning of its post-resurrection existence was the seeming failure of Jesus to live up to most of the expectations of the Messiah. There are, of course, ways out of this impasse. It can be argued that the Messiah has in fact appeared, but in a quite unexpected guise. Or it can be claimed that he has indeed accomplished what he set out to do, though most have not recognized the fact. Or it can be asserted that the apparent set-back is only temporary, and that he will return to fulfil his allotted task. It is a tribute to the Jewish origins of Christianity that all three of these moves were made. The Suffering Servant theology of the humiliated and dying messiah-figure is now the dominant Christian picture, though it represents virtually a complete *volte-face*. The hidden kingdom, present in our midst ever since the coming of Jesus, but unrecognized by the world, is a not unfamiliar thesis. And of course the whole elaborate theology of the second coming is in essence of response to the dashed hopes of the first.

But these were only temporary expedients. They served to establish continuity in the crucial early stages. But before long the church grew strong enough to carve out its own theology independent of any Jewish antecedents. Under the increasingly dominant influence of the Greek party an assessment of Jesus quite alien to Judaism and messianism developed. Where the Messiah had been seen as the forceful and irresistible agent of God's judgment and reign on earth, he now became the divine mediator between God and mankind. Rebellion – the principal metaphor for the disjunction between God and creation in the old scheme – was internalized in the form of ethical and moral sin. And where the cure for the former was the direct use of military might, the latter needed a mystery for its resolution: the mystery of the God-man. The accomplishment of this transformation from Messiah to Christ meant that the third expedient was unnecessary. Since Christ is the mediator, the atonement for our personal sins, and his kingdom is a kingdom of the heart and mind and soul, and since the paradigm for his effective mediation is the willing self-sacrifice of the innocent victim, there is no place any more for literal fulfilment of the messianic hope in terms like those of Revelation (essentially a collection of Jewish apocalyptic writings). This is why, of course, the last book in the New Testament has always been something of an embarrassment. It is irrelevant to de-Judaized Christianity, and is little more than a source of succour for the wild and undisciplined fringes of the faith. Calvin's dictum – that Revelation either found a man mad or left him mad – is precisely apposite.

The final twist in the tale was the application of allegorical and typological interpretative techniques to the Old Testament to force it to yield a hitherto unguessed-at store of christological treasures. With that move, Judaism was finally banished, and the Jews (in Christian eyes at least) barred from their own holy book! Only with the dawn of the age of historical criticism, the fading of literal belief in the incarnation of gods amongst men, and the recovery of something like a Jewish perspective on the Jewish scriptures, have we begun to see that the road the church took in the late first century was not the only one. We cannot, of course, go back. Nor would we wish to: the portrait of the suffering Messiah is too powerful and too true to experience to be discarded. It represents, I believe, a real and lasting religious insight which is ethically and theologically far superior to the apocalyptic messiah of the inter-testamental age. But while we cannot go back, we can hopefully recognize that this novel conception of messiahship signposts the beginning of a road which at least two communities – Jews and Christians – might dare to walk together.

The third item in our credal list about Jesus concerns his humanity. If it is true that the concept of his divinity is under discussion, and the rôle of mediator once allocated to him is less certain than in past days, it is still safe to say that the humanity and the historical reality of the life and death of Jesus are almost universally accepted. However, we must recognize that it is his *normal* humanity that is important. As soon as we move to such adjuncts as the virgin birth and immaculate conception, we are in territory which is wholly controversial. It certainly does not belong with the normal concerns of historical biography; and it would be no exaggeration to say that the great majority of serious biblical scholars judge the account of the virgin birth, and indeed the whole complex of infancy narratives, to be late, legendary, and derivative. There can be no grounds for including them within the terms of reference we have set ourselves, to find something like an acceptable core of Christian belief.

We come finally, under the heading 'On Jesus', to the statement of his resurrection, presence with God, and responsibility for judgment. Resurrection is of course a fundamental belief of

Christianity, and the resurrection of Jesus presents no philosophical problems not inherent in this belief in general. The records and reports preserved in the Gospels and Acts clearly indicate that, in the words of Joseph Heller, 'something happened'; exactly what that something was depends on how 'resurrection' is explained (bodily, spiritual, metaphysical) and the extent to which the various reports can be persuaded to yield anything like reliable historical information. In his book *Jesus the Jew*, Geza Vermes concludes that one basic irreducible fact remains – the empty tomb:

> In the end, when every argument has been considered and weighed, the only conclusion acceptable to the historian must be that the opinions of the orthodox, the liberal sympathizer and the critical agnostic alike – and even perhaps of the disciples themselves – are simply interpretations of the one disconcerting fact: namely that the women who set out to pay their last respects to Jesus found to their consternation, not a body, but an empty tomb.[8]

Regardless of how we may individually understand resurrection, there are a couple of things that need to be said about the resurrection of Jesus in particular, and what we may or may not deduce from it. In the first place, insofar as resurrection is the hope of all humanity, it cannot be used as proof of the special nature of Jesus: it is not something which distinguishes him from us – on the contrary, it is an element of his *human* nature. Indeed, to make resurrection a defining characteristic of Jesus's supposedly divine nature is to remove our hope. For it is because he was a man like all men that his survival of death has meaning for us. And in the second place, we should never forget that all our language about the life after death is necessarily metaphorical and speculative. When the early Christians sought to record their experiences of Jesus after Easter they used expressions of a mythic and figurative kind. It may well be that the only genuinely historical statement we can even theoretically make is 'the tomb was empty'. Perhaps a third *caveat* should be entered: could our faith in Jesus's defeat of death survive if, say, his body were to be discovered? After all, the natural processes of decay make it very clear that, whatever resurrection means for you and me, it cannot mean the reconstitution of the body we possessed at any stage of our earthly existence. That is a temporary shell, a vehicle of the soul's expression, not the essence of our being. Why should we imagine that Jesus was any more closely tied to his material body? As a matter of fact, some time ago a Canadian writer, Charles Templeton, produced a novel (*Act of God*) whose theme was the discovery of a grave in Palestine along with indisputable evidence that the body it contained was that of Jesus. Granted the basic improbability of this kind of certainty in the field of archaeological discoveries, Templeton's idea is an interesting one, and much of the tension of the novel derives from the reaction of church leaders to this most disconcerting piece of evidence. Unfortunately, he did not develop the theological implications beyond a very rudimentary stage; but his essential point is an important one, and it would be instructive to contrast the indecent haste with which the exorbitant claims of the Turin Shrouders are advocated with the probable response to the kind of uncomfortable historical 'fact' postulated by Templeton.

I do not propose to linger over the matter of the Day of Judgment. This belief belongs with the old apocalyptic messianic understanding of Jesus which seems to me to have been made redundant by the new conception of the purpose of the Christ worked out by the church. Judgment, like salvation, is individual and immediate, not communal and not held off till some mythic end-time.

What emerges, in conclusion, is that though we are agreed that Jesus is at the heart of our faith as Christians, it is hard to find any clear consensus as to the precise delineation of his importance. Chapter 5 was an essay at such a delineation which tried to spell out the consequences of dropping certain of the customary presuppositions. Whether it carries conviction will depend on the extent to which it is seen to be true to the life and teaching of Jesus himself, and to the essence of the Christian understanding of God. It does not really matter, in the end, whether one particular account finds general favour. What matters is that we should not lumber ourselves with unnecessary dogma and un-thought-out doctrine under the mistaken impression that we are thereby defending the faith. I hope that in the preceding paragraphs I have succeeded in showing that the faith is far more flexible and far more open than most of our systems and formulae are able to show. I will not presume to replace the list at the beginning of this section with a revised one of my own: that would be merely to perpetuate the false idea that human words can give final expression to divine mysteries. But if something in what I have said here and in Chapter 5 chimes with the experience of others, and makes it possible for *them* to form their own 'disposable' creed, I will be well pleased.

– 6 –

3. *Of the Spirit*

Of the creeds we are considering, the only one which discusses the Holy Spirit in any detail as an equal member of the Trinity is the Nicene. It is worth quoting for its very strangeness:

> We believe in the Holy Ghost, the Lord and Giver of Life, who proceedeth from the Father and the Son; who with the Father and the Son together is worshipped and glorified; who spake by the prophets.

There is a suspicion here of a somewhat desperate and artificial attempt to elevate the Spirit in the light of a theory of the Trinity. What we read in this passage does not appear at all to be a natural development in the way that the deification of Jesus was. The final clause is not at all a fair representation of the Old Testament understanding of prophecy, and we have noted above that the wording 'proceedeth from the Father and the Son' was controversial in its own day, and still remains so (if not incomprehensible). While the association of the Spirit with the act of creation is certainly scriptural, it would I think be stretching the biblical evidence to accord any autonomy to the Spirit in this sphere. It is strictly speaking God's instrument of life-giving; or perhaps better, simply a metaphorical way of speaking of God himself in his act of creating and sustaining life. And as to the idea that the Spirit is 'worshipped and glorified', I doubt if many in the reformed Christian traditions would find that a natural or normal part of the liturgy. Here, however, I must confess ignorance: it is quite likely that I am elevating to the level of a general principle something which is peculiar to me as an individual.

Be that as it may, I find the Nicene Creed to be distinctive in placing such stress on the nature and rôle of the Spirit. The Apostles' Creed, which devotes ten of its eighteen or so clauses explicitly to Jesus (and only two to God *per se*), does no more than mention 'the Holy Ghost' as one of a series of addenda to the declaration about Jesus which forms its core and essence. The three Scottish confessions, as we have noted already, *state* the doctrine of the Trinity, but effectively treat the Spirit as a means to various good ends rather than a person to be 'worshipped and glorified'. Thus where the First Article Declaratory speaks of 'worshipping one God', 'adoring the Father', and 'confessing our Lord Jesus Christ', when it comes to the third member of the Trinity the phrase used is 'trusting in' – and trust is to be placed, not in the Spirit directly, but in 'the promised renewal and guidance of the Holy Spirit'. This is a far cry indeed from the bold language of the Nicene Creed, but truer, I suspect, to the actual status of the Holy Spirit in Christian thought. The Bible itself quite clearly envisages the Spirit of God as analogous to the human spirit, and so in no way to be regarded as a separate being. Even John's Gospel, which makes so much of the promise of a Counsellor (his term for the Holy Spirit), is careful to specify that only when Jesus has gone can the Spirit appear (John 16.7). The Spirit is thus above all the way that God maintains his presence in the world, not a separate and equal being within the trinitarian pantheon.

We do not worship the Holy Spirit: we worship God. But within the limitations of our language and thought it is helpful to envisage God as working in our world through a power that we have some conception of. Phrases like 'the power of the human spirit' are not entirely metaphorical, and they offer us a starting point from which we have some chance of understanding the effective connection between the Creator and the creation. This is in fact the whole essence of Christianity: that the impossibly remote divine is at the same time inseparably bound up with the human. When we call Jesus 'Son of God' we are making use of an anthropomorphism to bring God within the compass of our thought world. This is perhaps obvious. Jesus shows us a God who, because he made us and because he is loving, can be thought of (without blasphemy) as being 'like' us. Perhaps this is the obverse of the Old Testament coin 'made in the image of God'. What may be rather less obvious is what I have been implicitly arguing in this section: that our language about the Holy Spirit is similarly anthropomorphic – a way of describing the deity and his/her actions in human terms. The Spirit reveals to us (as far as we are capable of understanding) how the God who is (unbelievably) 'like' us performs his/her great acts of love and salvation. Thus in the end Christianity – and this is its scandal – is a hopelessly anthropomorphic faith. The core truth of this religion is that human beings *per se* are effective metaphors for God. God becomes human – yes!! But it is precisely the point that no specific human being becomes God; for if Jesus is 'really' God the whole point is lost.

I suggested above[9] that we might see the Spirit as 'an expression of God's activity'. We can now spell this out more clearly. The Spirit is God active in the world, powerfully and effectively: it is, in other words, the realized expression of the will of God.

— 7 —

4. On Three-ness

In the beginning there was God.

Since that is quite literally a conversation stopper, any religion which believes it has some insight into the divine nature must at that point compromise. In the Old Testament a series of metaphors are used: God as creator, warrior, king, avenger, lover, father, mother and so on. Some of the metaphors almost take on a separate existence: Spirit, Word, Wisdom, Glory are the clearest examples.

What Christianity did was to embody the metaphorical. It was still possible to speak of the attributes of God, but in the final analysis all these metaphors were summed up in a real, flesh and blood, historical human being, Jesus of Nazareth. In him both of the moves made by the Old Testament were absorbed into one expression: Christ the living metaphor, separate from yet to be identified with the Creator. This then gave us the first of the three.

Because of the use of the idea of sonship to link Jesus and God, it was natural to select fatherhood as the most appropriate way to speak of God-in-relation-to-Jesus (and hence to all people). Of course it was not new to think of God as father. What *was* new was to think of God-as-father along with Jesus-as-son. So then there were two: the father and the son.

Although the Spirit could have been subsumed within either or both of the first two personae, the need for some way of referring to the continuing active divine presence in the human sphere led to its assuming a distinctive place in the metaphorical structure of Christianity. Besides, the conception of three has a long history as a religiously significant number, so that given the Old Testament's prior use of the Spirit as God's agent, it was but a small step to complete the triad.

From triad to trinity is another matter entirely. There is a rather satisfying symmetry about the pattern:

God the Father, Creator and Originator;
God the Son, revealing the Father;
God the Spirit, effecting the will of the Father.

But what is essential is that the common factor is God, and the rest is a means to an end, not an end in itself. Threeness is a metaphor; trinity is a metaphysical construct. There is one God, and one God alone. As Christians we approach that God through Jesus, who lives for us as an historical person in whom the knowledge of God reached that kind of peak which is only rarely found in human history. But he was not God. And in our day to day living we meet God in the encounter of spirit with Spirit; that which is of the essence of our humanity meets that which is of the essence of the divine. We say the Spirit of God finds us and enables our human spirit to rise above its earthly limitations. But that Spirit is not God. For nothing within the confines of created humanity can be God. Let us rejoice that we can find words to express the great mysteries of existence in terms we can understand. But let us ever beware of the blasphemy of thinking that these words describe more than the merest shadow of the reflection of reality. In truth, that is already more than we can comprehend.[10]

7

Practice

I

At this point I must assume that those who are still with me are at least prepared to reconsider their beliefs in the light of other faiths. The chapters devoted to Christian beliefs were intended to do two things: to demonstrate the scope for such reconsideration, and to say something – however incoherently – about my own convictions. It is by no means necessary to take on board my proposals in order to continue this study; I would think, however, that it is necessary to accept that it is possible to make such proposals. In a nutshell, dialogue is not a question of what ideas we accept, so much as recognizing that there are many ideas beyond our own limited philosophy which, however strange they may seem, have proved perfectly acceptable to other people.

We are now in a position to look at some practical steps. In Chapters 3 and 4 we sought to analyse attitudes to other faiths and the basic principles of dialogue in a somewhat theoretical way. Theory is certainly inevitable: no field of human endeavour is ever ploughed very effectively by purely haphazard techniques. But equally certainly, armchair theorizing will produce no crops. Only by trying them out will we discover how reliable or otherwise are the guidelines I have so far assembled. I have throughout assumed that dialogue is an intellectual pursuit, involving a high degree of awareness of the fundamentals of one's own faith and both the willingness and the ability to engage in a conversation about them in relation to what others believe. To put the matter thus may give the exercise a daunting aspect. Most believers are neither interested in nor able to take on such a far-reaching analysis of faith. And most encounters with other faiths take place, initially at least, either within the context of everyday life or in a practical religious situation such as mixed marriage. It is important therefore that dialogue should not be removed to a wholly esoteric realm where only professionals and pedants dare tread. This does not mean that we may resort to 'instinct' and 'common sense': what I said at the beginning of Chapter 4 still stands. But it does imply that the principles and attitudes advocated above may be applied at every level of intercourse. Let me give a practical, and not uncommon example.

The parents of a Jewish girl and a Christian boy who intend to marry would do well to understand the situation as one of dialogue, for otherwise fear, suspicion and a sense of betrayal will grow unchecked on fertile soil. Such a dialogue will be far from academic, which does not mean that it will lack depth. Indeed as both families face questions about their respective faiths and the practical implications of such a marriage, the opportunity is presented for a most profound meeting of hearts and minds, precisely because it is rooted in a real and vital human relationship. The potential rewards are enormous – both for the couple (if they take belief at all seriously) and for the families – because what is discovered and shared is actually lived out in an entirely practical way. Prejudice (probably hitherto unrecognized) can be exposed and discredited because the presence of real people shows up the caricatures of bigotry for the lies they always were. Fears melt away when it is seen that the object of those fears is not in the least fearsome! But because the rewards can be great, the dangers are correspondingly large. And because our instinct is to retreat from the unknown and take refuge in familiar 'certainties', the advantages hinted at above are all too rarely realized. All too often what happens in such circumstances is an entrenchment of the older generation's ill-considered first impressions, countered by the alienation of the couple involved. And this alienation, though at first expressed as antagonism to the elders and a determination to go ahead whatever the cost, not infrequently is transferred to the relationship itself, which becomes a microcosm of the very world of tribal superstition and bigotry which its existence was meant to challenge. Thus refusal on either part to risk a real meeting can actually increase hostility and prejudice, confirming all the worst suspicions of the mean minded in a kind of self-fulfilling prophecy. This is why what I argued earlier is of crucial importance. Those who face the practical problems of the multifaith culture *must* be made aware of the kind of fundamental principles which will give them a chance of success, and those who may have to counsel others in such circumstances ought also to be familiar with the ground-rules of dialogue.

It would be naive to suggest that good-natured, open-minded dialogue will dispose of all the difficulties of mixed marriage. The persistent failure of even the Christian denominations to sort out their differences should warn us against over-optimism. For many Christians in the West of Scotland, for example, the phrase 'mixed marriage' means marriage between a Catholic and a Protestant. The fact that this is still regarded as an inter-faith marriage is a perhaps shocking, but none the less salutary reminder of the need for realism. The meeting of quite different cultures in the context of a marriage, the different expectations of the two partners, and the problems of bringing up children in one faith or another (often resolved by leaving them bereft of all religious sensitivity) are familiar from the Protestant-Catholic connection. It does not take too much imagination to extrapolate to the situation where the two faiths involved are not even theoretically the same, where cultural differences have a geographical dimension, and where whatever decision is taken about the upbringing of children will likely alienate at least one family, and probably both. Dialogue, then, is not a substitute for knowledge, information, sound practical advice, etc. It will not give any answers about 'what to do with the children'. But it might well make it possible for the various parties concerned to share the problem and to recognize each other's point of view. This may not seem much; but it happens rarely enough to be highly esteemed if it can be achieved, and it can lead to deeper and closer relationships – something no amount of hectoring and manning of the barricades can ever do.

– 2 –

So far I have illustrated how dialogue might be used in an intensely practical situation. The remaining examples are of situations where there is no immediate pressing urgency, where dialogue can therefore be a more leisurely, reflective process. Perhaps this might be taken to mean that dialogue in these instances is an option that we can take or leave as we please. But this would be a mistake – as if to say that the only worthwhile medicine is sticking plaster for a bleeding wound. For the health and prosperity of the multifaith community it is not sufficient to wait for emergencies and then try to patch things up. By that time it is frequently too late to do any good, for the evil has become thoroughly entrenched. If the families involved in the first example had previously engaged in some form of dialogue in a non-stress situation, the crisis when it happened while not losing any of its urgency would have lost much of its threat. We will therefore take stock of how dialogue might proceed in three cases drawn from my own experience. They do not pretend to be more than a random selection: it would require a learned sociological volume to describe at all comprehensively those varieties of religious encounter which might deserve the description 'dialogue'. We can, for the time being, safely leave learned sociological tomes in the hands of learned sociologists and stick to our more limited objective. The case studies I have in mind are:

1. A dialogue involving mainly non-theologically trained lecturers in a university college in Pakistan.
2. The Sharing of Faiths movement in Glasgow.
3. An interfaith seminar held over a period of two years in the Divinity Faculty of Glasgow University, attended mostly by students in that Faculty.

These studies are not in any way full reports on the dialogues in question. I will in Chapter 8 give a more detailed analysis of one of them; but in the meantime we will look at the aims of each dialogue, the kind of people involved, the problems associated with the chosen procedure, and the achievements (if any) of the group.

— 3 —

1. Dialogue in Pakistan

This group met between 1969 and 1971 in Sialkot, a town in the Punjab about 70 miles north-east of Lahore. Politically it was a rather tense period, just after the fall of Ayub Khan, and during the military dictatorship of Yahya Khan. His regime ended in 1971 with the elections which brought Bhutto to power and saw the beginning of the tragic Bangladesh war. These tensions were reflected in the group, which had at one point to suspend its meetings when the Muslim participants experienced hostility from their compatriots over their meeting in this open way with Christians. Even those who took part in the dialogue were in the beginning, and for some considerable time, rather suspicious of the motives that lay behind the formation of the group.

The dialogue took place on the campus of Murray College in Sialkot, a Christian college affiliated to the University of the Punjab in Lahore. (The title Christian, by the way, meant that the college was run by a board of governors drawn from the Christian community. The student body was about 90% Muslim, and a good half of the teaching staff were also Muslim.) The dialogue was initiated by a member of the staff of the college who was both director of the sports department, and a pastor of the German

Lutheran Church. He had studied Islam in the course of his theological training, and his purpose in setting up the group was partly for his own interest and partly to see whether a Christian – Muslim dialogue could help in some way to break down the barrier of suspicion between the two communities. To this end he hoped to involve Pakistani Christians in the dialogue, and indeed to make it possible for himself and other expatriates to withdraw completely.

All those involved were lecturers, though only Martin Jaeger was a professional theologian. The discussion was therefore to some extent at an academic level, though strongly influenced by the element of personal commitment. For those who participated faith was a real and important thing; and being amateurs (in the true sense) they brought to the debate a liveliness that gave it a certain urgency, but also contributed tension – by no means always creative! – to the discussion. One factor which helped to make the dialogue possible at all was the social dialogue that already existed by virtue of the college being mixed Christian/Muslim. Members of staff were accustomed to meet in the common room and at formal dinners, where the fact of being a group of professionals engaged in the same task was of much more importance than any differences of culture, nationality or belief. We knew each other already, at a certain level, so that religious dialogue was not starting completely from cold. Certain introductory awkwardnesses could therefore be avoided. It would be relevant also to note that those who were interested enough in what was nominally their faith to take part in serious discussion of it were (as in any society) in a small minority. This contributed a certain subtle, probably largely unconscious unity to the group: we could identify a common enemy – the apathy of the great majority.

Some problems were inherent in the situation. Language was bound to be a barrier, for while we used English as our principal common tongue, I was in fact the only member for whom it was a native language. One spoke German, the Pakistanis used Urdu or Punjabi, and those participants who were skilled in the Qur'an knew it in Arabic! To some extent we could all use Urdu, but though that is the official language of Pakistan, it is not the native language of more than a small minority of Pakistanis. A second problem was posed by the conservative nature of both Islam and Christianity in Pakistan. To some extent this is a historical legacy. Pakistan was forged as a religious community in the teeth of opposition from the Congress Party, the British Government, and the Hindu majority, and it represented a response to genuine fears about the fate of Muslims in a Hindu state. It is hardly surprising then that in Pakistan the demands of Islam are strongly affirmed, and other religions, though tolerated, seen as distinctly inimical to the 'pure' faith. (The 'pak' in Pakistan means 'pure', and the name means 'land of the pure').[1] Christianity in its turn, being the faith of only a tiny minority (2%) of the population, is very defensive and dogmatic; and this is reinforced by the influence of the missionary movements in Pakistan (or in those areas of India which now form Pakistan), which largely followed an 'evangelical' rather than a 'liberal' pattern. The influence of certain of the more conservative American churches is particularly strong. These factors meant that the encounter between Islam and Christianity in Pakistan was more commonly confrontation than conversation. There was, on the whole, little precedent for dialogue. A third difficulty lay in the insistence by the Muslim participants that, at least in the beginning, the Christians taking part should all be expatriates. This was partly due to fears that the dialogue might turn out to be evangelism in another guise. While understandable, this restriction tended to undermine one of the fundamental objects of the meetings; and indeed, when a Pakistani Christian did join the group, it was at too late a stage in its lifespan to make much difference.

There is no doubt that the dialogue had beneficial results, though not of the kind hoped for in the beginning. The original objectives were, of course, far too grand. Half a dozen people meeting together could never hope to 'break down the barriers between the faiths'! We even failed to get much of a conversation going between individual Pakistanis of the two persuasions – for the Christian side was predominantly German and Scottish throughout the period of the group's existence. But at a much more modest level, things did happen. Ignorance was somewhat reduced. Tension was greatly eased. Individuals were changed, perhaps more than they realized at the time. I can testify personally to that, and this book is one of the indirect fruits of that anonymous and long-forgotten dialogue fifteen years ago. This is why dialogue is rarely popular: it is a long, slow, seemingly unrewarding process. It will never fill churches (or synagogues, mosques or temples for that matter), and affords no dramatic stories of conversion. Yet like the mustard seed which Jesus used as an analogy for the kingdom, it produces in the fullness of time a stronger and more substantial growth than the flamboyant but often short-lived blossom of the evangelical campaign.

– 4 –

2. *Sharing of Faiths in Glasgow*

In the early 1970s in Glasgow, Stella Reekie inspired and instigated the Sharing of Faiths movement. Largely through the force of her personality, and her deep and genuine love for people of all faiths and all races, she brought together Christians of various kinds, Jews, Muslims, Sikhs, Hindus, later Baha'is, and (somewhere on the fringe) Buddhists. Her vision was that these people of faith should literally share their faiths; that by meeting together, talking together, sharing together, learning together, and (who knows?) worshipping together there might grow bonds of fellowship and understanding that could contribute something towards the creation of a harmonious community of many faiths in Glasgow.

From her flat in Glasgow Street, which was also her office, her place of worship and a refuge for all manner of hungry souls, she created a community of faiths which has become an established part of Glasgow's character, and whose fame and influence have spread far beyond the Kelvin and the Clyde. From an early stage an annual Presentation was mounted which was intended to make available to the general public something of the flavour of the various faiths to be found in the city. In recent years this event has had official recognition, and has attracted, amongst others, parties of school children who seek out there – sometimes reluctantly, sometimes with amusement, and sometimes with evident interest – information to fill the gaps in their increasingly scanty knowledge about religion of any kind. It is a salutary experience to put in a spell of duty on the Christian stall and to discover that for a great many youngsters today Christianity is as mysterious and obscure an affair as Hinduism. Try explaining briefly the practice of the eucharist to a twelve year old Scottish pagan – it's a daunting task!

But this public presentation is really the least of the matter. Where the Sharing of Faiths idea gains its strength is in the regular meeting and working together of believers from different faiths. Working together on a committee, planning the shape of monthly meetings in the flat which will be taken in turn by representatives of each member faith, and co-operating in the task of communication: these are the effective core of the ideal. For it is about *sharing*, saying: 'Here is my faith, here is the shape of my belief. Can you go along with me at all? Can you understand me at all? Can we tread the road together, at least for a moment or two?'

This is the antithesis of conversion, though those who share are all strong believers. It is not intellectual dialogue, though many thoughtful people are involved. And it is not a kind of religious competition, though all who take part do so from a sense of the value of their own faith. The ideal from which the movement grew was of a coming together in community of people precisely in their distinctiveness and individuality. Out of that sense of difference there might develop an awareness of the great worth of each faith – an awareness, however, that could only grow and flourish when people actually met each other. Separately, in our well-defended corners, we can maintain that destructive mixture of fear and aggression which has been so often the mark of religious encounter. But when we sit beside, talk with, drink tea with, laugh with, argue with, plan with, share disappointments and victories with those whose way is not ours, we find that indeed a meeting takes place, a sharing occurs, in which our own belief is enriched through the strangely different faith of others. That is 'sharing of faith' – an intention rather than a programme, a hope rather than a set of aims and objectives.

Because of the way the movement developed in Glasgow, a great many people from a wide variety of religious and social situations have been touched by it at one time or another. The committee itself has had a remarkable continuity, with no wholesale changes, but at the same time a steady infusion of new members who have brought their own particular enthusiasms to bear. Obviously those who have belonged to that committee have been in a position to be quite deeply affected by the ideals it seeks to promote. The principal expression of the aims has been threefold: monthly meetings in the flat, open to all – but limited by the sheer space available; a yearly presentation, again open to all, and held in a public centre so that there is in effect no limit to the numbers who can attend; and occasional engagements to speak in schools and at meetings of various religious bodies. This last has been associated with the production of a limited amount of visual and printed information. As a result of these different approaches a considerable number of people have had at least a passing chance to see for themselves the reality of the world of faiths we live in today. To use the title of a tape-slide presentation produced by the committee in 1976, we live in 'A World of Difference'. The dissemination of a little information on a very wide front, though, is far from being the most significant achievement of the movement. Much more important is the fact that a small but growing number of people from all kinds of backgrounds have found that it is possible over a period of time to grow together with those of different faiths. This has been achieved mainly through the informality of meeting in a house in circumstances which made it impossible for too much dignity to be preserved! When a group of people share a floor a certain community of physical discomfort can produce a remarkable degree of spiritual and emotional intercourse! This is a less flippant observation than at first appears: quite a lot of our hesitation about other ways and other faiths arises from a feeling (unjustified of course) that the *people* themselves are 'different' – a feeling which is readily dispelled under the circumstances just described.

Like all movements, the Sharing of Faiths has been condemned by its own success to adopt certain institutional trappings, a fate which though deplorable is apparently unavoidable. The monthly events tend to have a fixed pattern to which now something of the nature of a tradition attaches. The annual presentation too, though illuminating and informative if you have never been before, has tended to settle into a very predictable shape. It could be argued that the most useful work now done is of an educational nature: talks to schools and other groups, dissemination of information, and so on. There may well be a significant correlation here with the phenomenon noted above, that in recent years an increasing percentage of visitors to the annual presentation has been represented by school parties.

By now it will be clear that a certain tension has developed between the kind of unstructured aims I claimed for the movement, and the rather formal nature of the threefold pattern described two paragraphs back. This forms a potentially fatal dissonance between means and ends: the need to use structured methods is in itself damaging to the free, unprogrammed nature of the desired sharing. Other problems arise, too, though of a less radical kind. For example, it would be disingenuous to pretend that everything is carried out in an atmosphere of mutual understanding and love! Arguments happen, perhaps one group suspects another is being publicly favoured. Complicated negotiations have to be conducted to dispel suspicion. Everyone involved is, after all, only too human. What is rather special about the movement in Glasgow, at least as I have known it, is that despite this the sharing continues. One other uncertainty ought to be mentioned. Over the years the monthly meetings have been presented in turn by the six faiths involved, usually interpreting in their own way a theme chosen for the year by the committee. Unfortunately this opens the door to a tendency for Christians to attend in force on 'their' day, Muslims on 'theirs', and so on. It will be readily seen that this is the perfect antithesis to 'sharing', and if it were to become a serious trend would threaten the very existence of the movement.

I have described the Sharing of Faiths movement in Glasgow because it is a good example of the way that dialogue can become relevant to people at a very immediate level. Despite the reservations just made, much has been achieved over the last twelve years, and much more may yet happen. All sorts of folk have met each other in what may best be described as a worshipful situation (even though formal worship may not have taken place: more on this in a later chapter), and have come to know that the differences between the faiths – which are still very real – are a lot less divisive than they once imagined. But there is only a certain amount that can be done by such means. For 'Sharing of Faiths' is explicitly *not* dialogue in the risk-bearing sense that we spoke of in Chapter 4; it does not engage at that level. The practical difficulties of creating a harmonious co-operation of six different faiths are not to be minimized: at times a most delicate balancing act is called for, and there can be no serious questioning of each other's fundamental beliefs in anything other than a very gentle and tactful manner. Nothing that could be seen as leading to a radical change in allegiance or to 'conversion' may be publicly endorsed. Of course private conversations of a more searching nature take place within the movement; but the ethos, the ambience of 'sharing' is of necessity one which gives a high priority to respect, courtesy and politeness. This is not a bad thing. Given the aims of the Sharing of Faith ideal, its limitations are inbuilt. For many people the approach to unfamiliar religions is difficult enough, so that the friendliness and lack of threat which the movement insists on are essential before the initial tentative steps can be taken. And the real achievement in getting six major religions to co-operate at all should not be undervalued. When the past and present history of Christians, Jews, Muslims, Hindus, Sikhs and Baha'is is considered only the Baha'is are innocent of having persecuted or fought with any of the others, and all have suffered at the hands of at least one. Worse still is the sorry record of bitter internal strife in certain faiths which is still producing a harvest of misery. In a limited way Sharing of Faiths is making a most important contribution to understanding and peace, and everyone who has become even a little more knowledgeable as a result of this movement represents a reduction in the potential for prejudice and therefore a small sign of hope for the world.[2]

– 5 –

3. Interfaith Seminar

My third case study deals with a group whose intention was to examine the possibility of dialogue rather than engage directly in it. Originally it was composed mainly of students and staff from the Faculty of Divinity in the University of Glasgow, and its aim was 'to examine how Christianity ought to react to, or let itself be influenced by the presence of other faiths in the same society'. Those involved were all to a greater or lesser degree engaged in full-time study of theological subjects, and the deliberate intention was to produce expressly theological guidelines which might go some way to prepare the ground for dialogue. The group met intermittently from May 1982 until April 1984 – whether it will continue is still an open question. At the start of 1984 it progressed from theory to practice, when a Muslim post-graduate student joined.

Theological students are nothing if not argumentative, and what very soon emerged was that it did not require the presence of different faiths for a dialogue to take place. The group spanned the widest possible range of Christian opinion, and illustrated many of the attitudes discussed in Chapter 3. Thus although the ostensible purpose of meeting was to prepare for dialogue with other faiths, what actually took place was a dialogue between sometimes irreconcilably different Christian views. One or two held the belief that if there is but one God, then two religions each claiming to worship one God must be in touch with the same God. But on the other hand there were those who could not accept any God outside Christianity as having any validity at all. Then again, at one extreme were a few who felt they had to insist on the claims of Christianity to be the final and unique expression of God's word to humankind, while others had no difficulty with the notion that Christianity was one faith among many, to be valued for its own particular contribution, but not to be exalted to a plane above all else. What was most interesting was the range of understanding of what it meant to be a Christian. This was not an explicit subject of discussion, but it quickly became clear that, far from all those present sharing some well-defined set of fundamental doctrines, the common element could be expressed quite simply as 'Jesus' – and beyond that the differences began.

Whether that is seen as a good or a bad thing, a sign of health or illness, will depend on the extent to which faith is measured by external standards like creeds and confession, or left to the individual's own conscience. Churches and sects being by their nature institutional tend to insist on the external: this is obvious enough, and needs no elaboration here. What is less clear is how these institutions can cope with the presence in their midst of those maverick spirits for whom doctrines are anathema and creeds the chains which fetter the soul. Presumably *some* kind of definition is necessary – maybe what the churches should be doing is seeking the minimum definition instead of, as is presently the case, trying to make long lists of theological statements for everyone to subscribe to. The evidence, such as it is, of the Interfaith Seminar is that where two or three are gathered together you will find at least as many theologies as participants in the discussion. (This kind of remark is often made to illustrate the argumentativeness of Jews; I see little evidence that Christians are one whit less disputatious than their Israelite cousins!) As an illustration of this not unfamiliar phenomenon, the next passage is composed entirely of remarks made in the group at one time or another: readers may draw their own conclusions about the likelihood of consensus in any gathering of more than one thinking Christian!

Christianity is unique, and the Christ-event necessary. Yet non-Christians will be saved.

There is a danger of emptying Christianity of all meaning and rendering dialogue too easy.

There is no point in unnecessary risk-taking in dialogue. Don't take risks with your faith, though no doubt faith is a matter of risk.

Jesus is God's final act of self-revelation. Thus Jesus is both chronologically and qualitatively the last revelation.

The significance of Jesus is that he *voluntarily* emptied himself of his rightful divine characteristics (Philippians 2.5–11). All other religious leaders, founders of great religions, retained some degree of self-interest – even the Buddha.

For me Christ is the best road, but I recognize other roads for others.

The more I see the truth in all religions the less I see the truth in any particular one.

Having picked up all the things you share from other faiths – are you still in the same religion with a deeper insight, or is it a different religion?

Tolerance is wishy-washy! What you believe matters a lot.

Fundamental to my beliefs is that there is one universal God who is responsible for the rich and varied creation in which we live, and of which we are all part. I am unwilling to believe that God has provided me with the means of knowing him simply because of the accident of my birth in a 'Christian' country, and has denied the means of such knowledge to others because they were not. Following from this I suggest that each nation, faith and religion differs only in its apprehensions and expressions of the one God, so that none are guilty of worshipping other or lesser deities. In other words, religious *expression* of God is dependent upon its location on the map, and its cultural environment.

The various differences which rapidly became clear were never reconciled. In fact what happened was that the group embarked on a Christian-Muslim dialogue without ever having worked out a clear rationale. Nevertheless the initial stages proved not without value; for although the original aim (to outline a theology for dialogue) remained a distant goal, the debate which had taken place proved to be a useful preparation. The sharp differences between Islam and Christianity, and the strength of conviction evident on the Muslim side, put the earlier inner-Christian differences into perspective. On the other hand, having already discovered that faith is a flower found in many different forms, the encounter with a confident and convinced Muslim was less breathtaking than it might have been. This dialogue is, at the time of writing, still at an early stage. Most of the discussion is by way of seeking and giving information, though a certain amount of probing and of supplementary questioning has ensued. The most interesting aspect for many of the Christians has been the discovery of what Muslims believe about Jesus – particularly the belief that Jesus escaped crucifixion and was transported directly to heaven. At one stage the challenge was offered, that if Christians would abandon the claim that Jesus was the 'son of God' there would be no gap between the two faiths. I suspect that, even granting the premise, there is a very long road to travel before reaching the conclusion: and it would be a road that both parties would have to travel together.

As an experiment in theorizing about dialogue, the Interfaith Seminar must probably be judged a failure: no theory emerged! There were also special practical problems associated with its location in a university setting: the periodic suspension of meetings at examination times, and over the long summer vacation, and the departure of students as they completed courses. These had the effect of making it difficult to engage on a sustained long-term project. Yet despite these reservations the group has made some progress, both in terms of the development of individual perceptions, and as a means of raising consciousness in a community where it is all too easy to be lost in the minutiae of Christian theology. If the Interfaith Seminar has made even a small impression on the propensity of theologians to strain out gnats and gulp down camels it will have justified its existence. But in the end the exercise of dialogue, however and wherever it occurs, needs no extraneous apology: it is its own justification.

– 6 –

The practice of dialogue is not easy. Quite apart from the intellectual and spiritual demands made on individuals involved – demands which they may find too exacting or too threatening – all kinds of local circumstances will conspire to make difficulties.

In the examples I have presented, however, the problems have not negated the worth of what was attempted. They may well have changed the aims formed at the outset, or demolished them completely. But dialogue is like that: the element of the unexpected is always present, and the openminded response always essential. Sometimes the very success of a group leads to a compromise: the Sharing of Faiths suggests that this is so, and that the compromise may well prove to be fatal to the basic aims of the group. The lesson of all three cases is that however we try to prescribe in advance the shape of a dialogue, the dynamics of the process itself will lead us in directions we never intended. What we are dealing with is an engagement between people which more often than not takes on a life of its own. The participants are not, of course, pawns in some cosmic game; but neither are they in full control of how the group develops, for that is a function of the interplay of individual personalities and aspirations within a group dynamic. Yet we must not simply abandon control and leave ourselves to float freely with the tide. Decisions have to be taken from time to time – to disband a group which has lost its purpose, for instance. Or to recognize when a transformed objective has ceased to be a truly dialogical one. Or to admit that practical problems have become an insuperable obstacle to advance. Dialogue must never be preserved on anything like institutional grounds: thus whatever multilateral church conversations may be, they are not dialogue, for the plain reason that they are formal and ecclesiastical.

No practical rules have emerged from this consideration of practical cases, except: be practical. There are no formulae for success, except: avoid all formulae. And no advice can be offered unless it is in the form of a word of encouragement: if you believe that dialogue is the way to break the power of ignorance, prejudice and fear, go ahead and do it. You won't persuade Christians to become Muslims, or Hindus to follow Christ. But a few people will as a result be wiser, more tolerant and more aware: there will have been a little more companionship on the way we all tread. That is a prize worth winning.

8

Anatomy of a Dialogue

The Christian

The idea of God as an old bearded man – the kind, just, almighty
ruler of the universe – is finished, apart from a few exclusive sects
who are fighting a rearguard action. We have to ask not only how
are our ideas about God to be expressed meaningfully, but also what
are these ideas, from where do we get them? The key is God, not
who 'exists' but who is 'met' – man to God, each partner equally
important.

Jesus – historically – is the place in which God shows what he is
like. Jesus reveals God to be a dynamic God who sets people free,
who asks us to love our fellow men, who allows us to be worldly.

What is the difference between a humanist and a Christian?
Perhaps none, if the humanist is good enough. Or the Christian!

The Muslim

God does not have meaning apart from his relations to men. He
has given to men certain powers to find their own way to God. His
dictates are made known to us through his messengers. The world
is a sort of examination hall.

In the Holy Qur'an, the Surah called 'The Beneficent' (Surah 55,
especially verses 1–25) refers to God's action in the world, raising
some and lowering others, ever watchful of all that is being done in
the universe. Those who embrace Islam are guaranteed prosperity
both in the hereafter and in the present – provided that we consider
prosperity in a collective sense. And at least the individual will
have peace in his heart.

God guides, directs, helps those who believe, and at the same
time watches to see how they stand up to difficulties. Every
thought, action, word and deed of ours is watched and recorded by
God, to be produced at the judgment.

— I —

In section 3 of Chapter 7 I described briefly a dialogue in Pakistan in the late sixties, as one of a series of examples. I want now, using notes taken at the time, to consider it in more detail. Thus instead of taking a cross-section of types of dialogue, as we did in the previous chapter, we will put one specimen under the microscope. The source for this study is a paper which I prepared a month or two after the last meeting of the group, based on notes taken at meetings and discussion papers used from time to time. This paper is incidentally quite revealing of the attitudes I held at the time — some of which now seem to me to be rather narrow and ill-judged, but of which I was then unaware. In the light of what has been said already about hidden presuppositions and prejudice, it is humbling to disinter from a past life (18 May 1971) documentary evidence of the truth of the old proverb about the pot calling the kettle black!

Besides witnessing to my own intellectual development (a subject on which judicious silence had best be observed), the style of the language is glaringly pre-feminist. The two passages quoted at the beginning of this chapter would quite rightly be rejected by any sensitive editor today for their use of sexist language. I can only plead for sympathy for what was written then on the grounds that the sexual revolution was not even a gleam in the eye of the *Zeitgeist* at that time in Pakistan. I will also plead the right to quote without the form of the quotation (even if it was my own work) being taken as evidence for my latter-day views. And lastly, it is instructive to remember that this was a dialogue without women (a necessary consequence of the social and religious mores of the country it took place in), so that sensitivity to the feminine aspect is hardly to be expected. If that leads anyone to judge harshly what went on in the group, or to dismiss its 'inklings' as irretrievably flawed, so be it. I can only plead that hindsight would be a fine thing, if we had more of it at the time.

The two definitions of God at the beginning of this chapter were given during a meeting in 1969, after the group had been meeting for several months. They reflect fairly well the general position of the two sides in the dialogue. The Christian synopsis, viewed from the contemporary scene, is over-optimistic in its belief that the old-fashioned picture of God is virtually dead. Indeed, I suspect that the majority of present-day conservative Christians would be much happier with the Muslim definition, in which 'Islam' could be replaced with 'Christianity' and the reference to the Surah with a suitable biblical text to give a rather orthodox statement of faith! At one extreme, the two portraits are very different; the first appeals to the possibility of a worldly Christian and a humanism which could be superior to Christianity, while the second is uncompromising in its insistence on adherence to Islam and on the reality of judgment. Yet there are also important points of contact. Both speak of God being 'met', of his being known only through his relations with men and women (*sic*). Both recognize our need for help: the first finding it in the historical person of Jesus who shows us what God is like; the second seeing it in God's direct guidance, direction and help. There are, then, sufficient grounds in these two statements for continuing the dialogue, but clear indications that a real gulf exists in how God is perceived, both in himself and in his relation to humanity. As a matter of fact this pattern was borne out in the actual development of the group.

— 2 —

The context and conditions of the dialogue have, I think, been sufficiently dealt with in Chapter 7. What we must now do is to follow the progress of the group through various stages of its existence.

1. At the beginning there were four Muslims and one Christian participating, the latter being the one who instigated the dialogue. This imbalance, and the lack of any members of the indigenous Christian community, was at the express request of the Muslims, who were to some extent uneasy about the motives behind the group and the methods that might be used. Clearly there was some fear that it might be a cover for some kind of Christian evangelistic effort — a fear which, though unfounded, was understandable in the light of the particular character of the Church in Pakistan. With these conditions, meetings began in January 1969, taking place once a fortnight.

Generally speaking, in this first stage a pattern was established of questions from the Christian side and answers from the Muslims. It soon became apparent that they were working on the assumption that Martin Jaeger had founded the group in order to learn about Islam, and that their task was to enlighten him. Indeed, when it became known that he had read books about Islam and had studied the subject quite extensively, they were surprised, and wanted to know why, if he already knew about Islam, he had found it necessary to gather the group together! There was at this early stage no sense of the reciprocity of dialogue, no feeling of any need on the Muslim side to increase their knowledge of Christianity and Christians.

It was also natural that at the beginning there should be some tension, and a danger of misunderstanding – a danger compounded by the fact that the discussion was carried on in English, a language which at that time was not the native tongue of any member of the group. For example, at one point, Martin Jaeger, translating a German idiom rather literally into English, spoke of something being 'against God' (where 'in front of' or 'before') would have been more appropriate. Without his realizing it, this was picked up by the others in the group as a dishonouring of God; and until the misunderstanding was removed a distinct awkwardness made itself felt. As time went on, of course, these initial tensions began to ease, and misunderstandings less of a problem, so that discussion became freer (despite the rather dogmatic approach of one of the Muslims). An attempt was made to explore the shape of personal belief amongst the Muslims, without much success since each asserted that Islam was a community and social matter rather than an individual one: what the community as a whole assents to is of far greater importance than the faith of any one individual. Of course this is not the whole picture, and we will see how as time went on certain other dimensions emerged.

To sum up the first stage, then, it might be fair to say that it was concerned more with 'facts' than with opinions; more a matter of question and answer than dialogue; and had to face the problems arising from tension and misunderstanding before any attempt could be made to explore together the meaning of faith.

2. After a few months, in March 1969, I joined the group. By this time they had relaxed somewhat, and felt able to widen their terms of reference. Discussion, however, was still fairly formal, often focusing on the technicalities of some specific Islam doctrine in reply to questions or exploratory statements from the Christians. (The passage quoted at the beginning of the chapter is from this period.) Questions still did not come freely from the Muslims, who seemed to prefer to let their contribution be in the form of responses to other initiatives, and there was still a noticeable atmosphere of restraint – doubtless at least partly attributable to my presence.

We decided after a few meetings that in order to break the rather formal pattern of the dialogue so far it would be beneficial if each member in turn gave a brief account of their own faith. If this was done honestly it would give the discussion a more personal dimension and dissipate to some extent the theological smoke-screen which had up till that time prevented any real engagement. The difficulty and the real challenge involved in such an exercise should not be underestimated: it tends to leave the individual vulnerable, since it removes from him or her the protection of the group, and is for that reason somewhat threatening. Despite this, the exchange of 'testimonies' took place, and proved to be something of a turning point in the history of the dialogue.

One of the Muslims said that he was not basically a religious-minded man, but that, conscious of the problems of life, he had sought for some answer and had found in Islam what he was looking for. His experience – one familiar in the Christian milieu also – was that there was a real practical advantage to be gained from taking one's faith seriously: Islam turned out to be, for him, relevant to his life in a very practical way. If you like, this was an example of the plain man's approach to Islam – a personal appropriation of the faith which is nominally that of the whole culture, without appealing to any solemn or tendentious theological apparatus. His testimony was a striking reminder of the oneness of humanity and the universality of our hopes and fears.

By way of contrast, another of the Muslims spoke of his belief in much more theologically structured terms. He was an older man, who had studied deeply in his faith, and for him therefore it was natural to refer to the wider teachings of Islam in speaking of what mattered to him personally. Islam is of course a strongly community-centred religion, and this came across in what he said. He believed firmly in the historical relevance of Islam, and saw it as having a definite political dimension: you could not separate religious from social, national and political hopes. He looked forward to (and believed in) a time to come within this world's history when, under Islam, all would be perfect. The model and analogy for this hope was to be found in the period under the first few caliphs when (he believed) Islam had been perfectly manifested in the Arab nation. In particular he hoped for at least a partial vindication of this hope in the not too distant future in Pakistan by means of political action on the part of Islamic political parties.

It is very clear that what drew these two men to Islam were very different things. While the first gave expression to motives we could readily recognize from our own experience, the second spoke in terms which it would be very hard for post-reformation Christianity to endorse. We make a very sharp distinction between the sacred and the secular, and tend to frown (particularly in Protestant circles) on the church's being involved in 'politics'. It was not always so. The idea of Christendom was an intensely political one, and the whole purpose of the Crusades (a particularly appropriate example in this context) was to create a Christian kingdom in competition with the Muslim states of the middle east. We have seen something of a return of the political dimension in Christianity in recent years, with the involvement of religious leaders and lay people in the peace movement, in human rights and third world issues, and in the freedom struggles in Africa and Latin America. The fact that this has happened reminds us that the Muslim concept of the identity of 'church' and 'state' is not so alien as we might suppose; on the other hand, the simple equation made by Islam could never be endorsed by Christianity. There is at the root of the latter faith a powerful dichotomy between the institutions of human political power and the practice of faith. This is why Christians in politics tend to be in opposition, if not in outright revolt, while the world today contains several examples of explicitly Muslim states (that is, states which are ostensibly governed according to Muslim law). We have in recent years seen Iran change from being a secular, Westernized state, to a fundamentalist Muslim one; and the hope, expressed by the second Muslim in that dialogue in 1969, that Pakistan might become a genuinely Islamic state has also been fulfilled to the extent that that country, too, has a government which claims to be faithful to the precepts of Islam. It is also a military dictatorship, which must to some extent reduce the achievement. It is difficult sometimes for secularized Westerners to understand the forces which lead to the formation of what to us appear to be narrowly religious regimes in the Muslim world. Perhaps there is something to be learned from the testimony of that man in Sialkot fifteen years ago.

The Christian testimonies came as something of a surprise to the Muslims. For they reflected, not the conservative religion of the Pakistani church, but the liberal, non-dogmatic pattern of mid-twentieth-century European Christianity. This provoked a response from the Muslims, who wanted to know what dogmas the Christians would consider to be essential. This was felt to be a question that could not be answered, since dogmatic definition was something alien to the way in which they experienced their faith. Here a real gulf opened up between the fundamental indefinability of the Christian position and the essentially dogmatic character of the Muslim. It must of course be stressed that dogmatism and definition is by no means alien to Christianity. Most churches (as we have already seen at some length) subscribe to creeds, confessions and statements of faith. But by a fortuitous combination of time and circumstances those involved in the dialogue were particularly reluctant to be tied to *any* formulae at all. To some extent this was a reaction to the extreme conservatism of the church in Pakistan; a feature, therefore, of the cultural context of the dialogue.

3. After the summer of 1969 the group did not meet for several months, and it was not until the spring of 1970 that we got together again. There had been trouble in the college of a religious nature, and without doubt some pressure was exerted on the Muslim participants. Certainly while the disturbances continued the dialogue could not resume, and one member dropped out (because of age, the difficulty of travelling at night, and fears of reprisals from his neighbours). But when it became possible to meet again it was interesting that the others were prepared to take part. Even more significant was the fact that from the beginning the atmosphere was very relaxed, as if a relationship based on friendship rather than merely on common religious interest had developed. Indeed, we found it possible to discuss the conflict in the college openly, and to criticize on both sides the different stands being taken by the two communities at the time.

We took up again the matter of dogma. Can we or should we be able to draw up a list of the essential doctrines of the faith? No basic change had taken place in the views expressed above; but at this point the question of the sources of dogma arose, and so we turned our thoughts to the holy books of Christianity and Islam. Once again the fundamental difference in approach was apparent: on the one side, the application of the methods of biblical criticism to the text of the Bible; on the other, the use of an extremely literalistic interpretation of both Bible and Qur'an. At this stage I would like to record the substance of what was a recurring discussion on the nature of the Bible and the Qur'an, and the person of Jesus – a discussion which, as we shall see, had serious implications for the development of the dialogue. It should be remembered that what follows is not meant to be a definitive statement of the teachings of either Christianity or Islam on these matters. It is strictly speaking what was communicated within that group, and is necessarily limited by the knowledge of those taking part, and the accuracy of my records.

The teaching of Islam is that from Adam to Jesus God kept sending prophets whose original message was pure Islam, but whose teaching was corrupted and lost with the passage of time. Thus the Jews, who have the Old Testament prophets in common with Islam, and the Christians, who share in addition the prophet Jesus, are both in the line of succession of Islam. The Old Testament (the *shari'at*) and the New Testament (the *injil*) are both foreshadowings of the perfect and infallible word of God which is the Qur'an, finally and for all time revealed by means of the prophet Muhammed. Consequently the adherents of all three faiths are looked upon by Islam as 'the people of the book', and are held to be closer to Allah than those of any other faith. We have in common the worship of the One God – which is the central tenet of Islam.

This teaching has the obvious consequence that if we want to discover the truth about Judaism or Christianity we may find it in the Qur'an, which is the perfect revelation of God to mankind. If we want to know what Jesus really wanted to teach us, the answer is 'Islam'. For a Muslim, this is dogma: the Qur'an is perfect; the Qur'an teaches us that Jesus was a prophet of Islam; therefore what Jesus originally taught was Islam, which teaching was later corrupted by his disciples and by the Christian church. Hence if we seek to discover the authentic voice of Jesus what we will hear is the voice of Islam.

Within the modern biblical critical movement there are tools which might make it possible to verify this claim by Islam. For the aim of the scholarly study of the Gospels over the last century has been, recognizing that the New Testament is biased towards a church interpretation of events, to recover as far as possible the original teaching and actions of Jesus. Since the Muslim view is that this original teaching was identical with the teachings of the Qur'an, a comparison of the conclusions of biblical criticism with the main tenets of Islam should be suggestive. Yet what emerges from this scientific study is a Jesus who has little time for legalism and superficial morality, who placed the laws of purification very far down his list of priorities, who associated freely and without condition with sinners and the worst kind of social outcastes, and who spoke of a God who could be directly and immediately encountered by any who sought him. His teachings cannot be made to yield any code of conduct or list of laws for the regulation of the Christian community; in this he is very different indeed from Muhammed. For the Qur'an is believed to be a complete and comprehensive guide to every aspect of life; within its pages are all the laws we need for our guidance. In fact, if we study the way in which the church developed, it was a development *towards* rather than away from an Islamic-type community. Institutionalized Christianity has a surprising amount in common with Islam and rabbinic Judaism. It is the free, unstructured approach of Jesus which runs counter to all these religions, with its emphasis on faith not as belief in a set of rules, but as a meeting with the living God.

The effect of this discussion was to leave us in something of an impasse. The firmly-held belief of the Muslims in the group and the equally determined faith of the Christians had come into headlong collision, and it seemed at that point that no matter how long – and with however much good will – we knocked at these particular doors, we would make little impression. We felt that our theoretical discussions had reached a stage where they could not fruitfully go forward. Accordingly we decided that the next step should be to approach some practical problem in common, or look for some area where we had a shared opinion. Having spent a good deal of time analysing and discussing our differences, could we not now seek to find the maximum possible area of common concern, common action, common belief? Unfortunately at this time fate once again interrupted the course of the dialogue when we had to suspend meetings for about six months owing to a disruption of college routine caused by the elections of December 1970.

4. In January 1971 the last series of meetings began. The election which brought Bhutto to power (and was to lead to the break-up of Pakistan) had taken place, and we spent some time discussing the implications. The atmosphere was very relaxed: all signs of the original tension seemed to have disappeared. It was now possible to introduce a Pakistani Christian to the group. After one or two meetings largely devoted to picking up the threads we agreed to take up the approach agreed on the previous summer. That is, some common ground would be sought, whether theoretical or practical. The first attempt was made by one of the Muslims, who felt that we could reach agreement on belief in the One God. Since the Qur'an recognizes that we are all 'people of the scriptures', it is fitting that we should talk together about our common belief in God Almighty, the one and only Lord. Since this is a central belief for Jew, Christian and Muslim alike, it might afford a basis on which to build some kind of unity. Doubtless there are differences in the way we come to know God. For the Muslim it is through the divinely revealed Qur'an, and for the Christian it is through the life and teaching of Jesus. This is really no barrier from a Muslim point of view; for Jesus is recognized as a prophet of Allah who taught and lived Islam, only to have his message distorted by the church. That later distortion, however, does not invalidate his teaching or his life.

Unfortunately, as we have already seen, this brings us to a sticking point. The Christian view was that Jesus in fact showed us aspects of God somewhat different from those stressed in Islam. Although we could certainly agree on the oneness of God, the emphasis placed on Jesus and the way we understood his revelation tended to be divisive. Since there is inevitably a close link between our concept of the deity and the way that concept is mediated, the differences between a Qur'anic and a New Testament account of God become more than superficial. Everything we say about God apart from asserting his uniqueness and unity is subject to the kind of differences which the two modes of revelation entail.

From this rather inconclusive discussion we moved – and this, as it turned out was the last of our meetings – to a consideration of various possible practical steps. The bulk of what now follows was presented to the group in the form of a paper.

If we cannot agree on the nature of God, is there any other dogmatic ground on which we might find a consensus? It would seem unlikely, if it is indeed true that the basis of Christianity is radically un-Islamic; for we are only likely to find common doctrinal ground on relatively trivial and unimportant points.

One other area of common ground may be mentioned only in passing, for it does not really help us much with our present problem. We of course have a common interest in learning about each other's faith and understanding each other as fellow men. But if we stop at merely learning and understanding we miss the point of dialogue, through which we hope to come closer than simply viewing each other, however sympathetically, from opposite sides of the fence.

There remains the practical approach, which might still prove fruitful. Let us sink our dogmatic differences and seek to work together in some of the practical problems of human life. For as human beings making common cause to set right some universally recognized evil, surely we can find much of a practical nature that we can share, and so perhaps learn to share at a deeper level also. Take an example. We probably all agree that the threat of overpopulation is one the world ought to be trying to deal with. On present trends the world will have too many people by the end of this century; even now certain areas are more densely populated than their resources can afford. In particular, look at the plight of a poor man with seven or eight children for whom he cannot find enough to eat. What can we do together to help? It is not hard to see that however well-meaning we may be, certain dogmatic positions will soon make themselves felt. Some say contraceptives are contrary to God's will; others claim that unless we use family planning devices the problem will never be solved. But until we have reached agreement on the dogmatic issue, we cannot act together. Separately we can each do our bit. But before long some matter of principle asserts itself, and we cannot wish it away. In economics, for example, where we might want to use investment as a means of increasing what meagre wealth is available, some will argue on religious grounds that banking should be interest-free. Impasse!

The problem seems to have turned full circle. Last week we felt that if we concentrated on dogma we would be forever arguing about points of difference, rather than finding common ground. Now, if what I have said is correct, we find that we cannot effectively put principle to one side and opt for practical action; for just when we think we are getting somewhere together the doctrinal issue has to be faced.

The problem outlined in these notes was discussed at some length, though without any definite conclusion. Both Muslims and Christians considered the idea of the meaning and the spirit behind law and dogma, and expressed their shared conviction that in spirit a way might be found, despite the barriers of doctrine. That such an agreement could be expressed was in itself a victory for the dialogue: those who had begun two years' earlier with a burden of uncertainty and some suspicion now knew that there was a desire for community which transcended the overt differences that none of us would have wished to belittle. And at the end of the day the success of dialogue rests not in its programmatic achievements or its array of doctrinal syntheses, but in the coming together as friends of those who were once strangers.

– 3 –

It seems somehow perverse to append conclusions to an organism as undefined as a dialogue. Its formal meetings may end, but its growth goes on, with echoes and implications for a future that cannot be guessed at. In 1971, when the first report was written, I said:

This is essentially a descriptive report. I have made no attempt to list specific conclusions or to make general prescriptions for dialogue. If certain points seem to arise from this report which are worthy of note, of discussion, or of refutation, that is good. If no such points arise that is also good. For this report is not an attempt to dissect a corpse, but to give a lively picture of a living body.

The very existence of this book shows that I have abandoned the claim to be avoiding general prescriptions for dialogue. And the writing of the present section would seem to be precisely an attempt to list specific conclusions. For both of these lapses I ask the reader to forgive me, and if preferred, to move directly to Chapter 9! Yet the gap in time and space between that dialogue and the present world perhaps justifies the addition of a few supplementary comments.

The initial tensions in the group were noted several times. It should be recognized that the whole concept was fraught with difficulty for those Pakistani Muslims who participated. They were opening themselves to misunderstanding, and possibly to criticism, in a situation where civil disturbance was a daily occurrence, and religious feelings prone to run high. That they took part at all says much for their character and integrity. That they were able to reach a certain rapport with Christians from a wholly different culture and talk as frankly as they did is its own tribute to the openness and acceptance that can be found even in as closely defined a religion as Islam. I suspect that the Muslim faith is one of the least understood in Britain today: if this record of a past encounter encourages others to embark on a similar project, that alone will have justified the enterprise.

It hardly needs to be said that the universal nature of human concerns was a constantly present theme of the dialogue. We do have a tendency when thinking of inter-religious debate to put people in little boxes called 'Muslim', 'Christian', 'Hindu', etc., and to impose the resulting caricatures on those with whom we talk. Even if that is present at the start of a dialogue – and it often finds expression in remarks like, 'But I thought *all* Muslims believed . . .' – it should rapidly disappear once a few meetings have taken place. What is perhaps more important is to realize that this is an insight we desperately need to share as widely as possible.

Perhaps it should also be noted that it can take quite a while for everyone involved to grasp the ethos of dialogue. For the whole of the first stage of the Murray College dialogue it seemed that the Muslims were under a misapprehension about what was going on, regarding it as something like an educational class for Christians to learn about Islam. It is not necessary – indeed it would be grotesque – for participants to attend a briefing session on 'Principles and Practice of Dialogue'; but there has to be a high level of awareness within the group. Not only do you have to take part, you have to watch yourselves taking part.

Since the analysis has now reached the stage of watching oneself watching oneself taking part, it may be fitting to close now, before falling into an infinite regression. For though dialogue is an on-going, open-ended affair, its local manifestations are strictly limited in scope. The waves come and go, ebb and flow, but the sea is always there, an inexhaustible resource.

9

Dissonance

Many Christians, sincerely concerned to be true to their faith, but desiring also to take seriously the claims of dialogue, find themselves facing a genuine dilemma: how can the call to mission be reconciled with dialogue as we have outlined it in earlier chapters? I want in the next few pages to consider this conflict in the light of the psychological theory of *cognitive dissonance*, which offers, I believe, a useful way of describing the dilemma, and might help to explain why dialogue (despite its irenic intentions) so often provokes antagonism and condemnation.

— I —

Christianity, like Islam, includes a clear missionary imperative. Because of the uncompromising nature of this demand, there is an inherent dissonance between dialogue and the call to mission. To allow the possibility of the former is tantamount to an admission that in some circumstances it may be right to ignore the great commission of Matthew 28.19–20:

> Go and make disciples of all nations, baptizing them in the name of the Father and of the Son and of the Holy Spirit, teaching them to observe all that I have commanded you; and lo, I am with you always, to the close of the age.

Yet if we adopt this Matthean commandment as the only form of our response to other faiths we are left with nothing to say when the gospel (as we have presented it) fails to make any impression. We are forced into either arrogance or defeatism: either *we* are failures or our hearers are damned. Such seemingly clear-cut distinctions are meat and drink to those who wish to keep the gospel simple and root out any tendency to indulge in independent thought. The secret of all such argumentation, and the weakness of it, is that certain assumptions are carefully hidden in order to force a choice between equally unpalatable alternatives. 'Have you stopped beating your wife yet? Answer yes or no!' 'Which would you rather be: Red or dead?' 'When Jesus claimed to be the Son of God he was either mad, a liar, or speaking the truth.' In each of these examples there is information lacking, or the question is phrased in such a way as to preclude certain middle positions. This style of rhetoric is analogous to the logical principle known as the *excluded middle*: if A is true, then the negation of A must be false. Or, in a more extended form, if all the possibilities are represented by A, B, C . . . P then it is impossible for Q to be true. Now in very elementary logical problems it may be possible to apply such a simple procedure. But it is a most unsatisfactory tool for the analysis of real situations, for the obvious reason that it can virtually never be claimed that all the possibilities have been identified. Thus the question about Jesus (an old favourite of the fundamentalists, by the way – it is still being used by Billy Graham) is invalid because there is at least one further conceivable alternative: that he never claimed to be the Son of God. Unfortunately for the polemicist, to introduce that fourth option is to evacuate the original formula of all its force.

I said that this kind of argument has both strength and weakness. Its weakness is that even an elementary consideration of what is being said will uncover the concealed agenda. Its strength is that very many people simply take what is said at face value, and thereby find themselves forced into agreeing – albeit reluctantly – with the speaker's claims. Of course we can't say that Jesus was mad or a liar – that would be unthinkable. Therefore he must be divine! And in the case with which we began, there is a strong temptation to adopt some sort of doctrine of the (self-willed) condemnation of the unbeliever because the alternative (that the gospel is weak and ineffectual) is even worse to contemplate. Fortunately human beings not infrequently preserve a certain modesty and ability to recognize hubris, with the result that there has always been a tradition which questioned the absoluteness of the missionary claim and the automatic rejection of those who refuse to respond. Indeed, when the modern missionary movement began it was regarded with considerable suspicion in orthodox Christian circles. Some, from a strongly neo-Calvinist position, were content to leave damnation to God. Since everything was in any case doubly predestined, there was a certain arrogance in human beings presuming to do the work of God in communicating the gospel. Others simply perceived that those who endorsed the missionary programme were both enthusiasts and eccentrics, and therefore to be kept decidedly on the fringe. (Those enthusiasts and eccentrics who evangelized closer to home – most notably the Methodists – were in fact edged right out of the established church altogether.) I do not seek to defend either neo-Calvinism or apathy. The representatives of these two groups resolved any possible dissonance by a technique of avoidance: they lived in a 'Christian' country in which there was obviously no call for mission; and the rest of the world impinged rarely enough to be of no consequence. But the great explosion of missionary endeavour in the later nineteenth century, coupled with the creation of the British Empire, brought a wider world into the direct consciousness of many more people. Now the great divisions in religion could no longer be ignored, and mission moved from the fringe to the very centre of the church's activity. Most of the great missionary societies were founded in the second half of the nineteenth century (as the spate of centenary celebrations in the last two decades will testify), and for the better part of a century the dominant Christian belief was that in due course the world would be 'won for Christ'. Dissonance between expectation and actual achievement was minimized. To be sure there still remained a great many who resisted the appeal of the Christian message, but by a kind of sleight of hand any decision about their fate could be deferred while the great advance continued.

The extent to which missionary success was bound up with the colonial enterprise only began to become apparent in the sixties, as more and more former colonies became independent countries, and there was no particular social or political advantage to be gained from embracing a religion closely identified with the former ruling class. By this time it was clear that mass conversions were the exception, and that where they had occurred it was very often from the ranks of a socially and economically depressed class. Moreover, independence brought with it a much sharper awareness of the traditional religion of the community, with the result that some of them have experienced something of a renaissance within the last fifty years. Hinduism in India and Islam in India, Pakistan and North Africa show no signs of withering away. If anything the experience of having been intensively evangelized for a hundred years by Christianity has stimulated these faiths to a fresh enthusiasm and vitality. (This may in truth be the one lasting contribution of the missionary movement – to have acted, as it were, like the grain of sand which provokes the oyster into producing a pearl; and it is no mean achievement.) Even in those parts of Africa where the dominant religion is still Christianity, a characteristically African form of the faith has often developed, and has broken quite radically with the established and traditional churches of the West. And in the West Indies the recent popularity of Rastafarian sects shows that this trend is by no means dead. It cannot be denied that Christianity has taken root in many places: the real success story is probably Africa; but the recent re-emergence of the Christian church in China after decades of secret existence has been a dramatic revelation. Of course the Christian community is still a tiny minority in that vast land, but it is surely one that is now thoroughly indigenous, and likely to survive.

Let me try to bring all this into perspective. It would be very easy to make fun of the post-reformation missionary movement, with its sublime identification of Christianity with English social conventions and moral priorities. The fact that it became very much identified with the imperial ideals of the Victorian age – an identification which missionaries themselves quite consciously encouraged – has rendered it irredeemably suspect in this (so-called) post-colonial era. Yet most of those involved were honest and sincere, and many did genuinely care for the people amongst whom they worked, seeking to improve their material as well as their spiritual lot.[1] To hold a conviction strongly and to wish to share it with as many people as possible is entirely natural. Moreover there is a long and honourable tradition of itinerant preachers, scholars and wise men whose calling is to travel the world both seeking and imparting truth. Where the enterprise becomes misguided is in its claim to have the *one* truth that will convince the *whole* world. Had I not denounced the style of argument a few paragraphs ago I would be tempted to say that such a claim is either madness or arrogance! However, let me observe more judiciously that its effect was to put the church in general and individual missionaries in particular in a rather nasty cleft stick. For the world has all too clearly not been convinced, and would appear to be further away than ever from that ideal goal. And so we return to the dissonance already identified:[2] either we have failed as missionaries or the world is damned.

$$-\ 2\ -$$

I have referred several times to the experience of dissonance. In recent years the psychological theory of cognitive dissonance has been applied in a number of religious studies, notably by Leon Festinger in a study of a group which predicted the end of the world 'and lived to contemplate the failure of that prediction'; and by Robert Carroll, who applied the theory to the failure of expectations in Old Testament prophetic traditions.[3]

The theory, in the form which is of interest to us, deals with the conditions under which a group may hold a belief which is capable of direct disconfirmation, and the reactions of the group when such a disconfirmation takes place. The whole of Carroll's second chapter[4] is devoted to a discussion of the theory, and the presentation which follows is greatly indebted to that chapter, which offers a particularly clear and helpful analysis of cognitive dissonance. (The source of each direct quotation is identified by the page number immediately after it.) How the theory relates to dialogue and mission will, I hope, become apparent as we proceed, and will be spelled out in detail in due course.

To begin with, an introductory definition. 'Cognitive elements are the basic units of dissonance theory. . . . Conflict occurs when a person has to make a choice among a number of possibilities, each of which offers a desirable option. Once the decision has been made the possibility of experiencing dissonance is created. . . . In Festinger's terminology dissonance is a replacement term for inconsistency, so that instead of behaviour, beliefs or opinions being inconsistent with each other they are now said to give rise to the experience of dissonance. Cognitions are what people know, believe or feel . . . so cognitive dissonance arises when two cognitions are inconsistent with one another' (p. 87). Obviously no group or individual begins with a set of mutually inconsistent beliefs – or at least, not consciously. Religious structures are designed to provide the kind of comprehensive account of 'life, the universe and everything' which answers all questions and questions no answers. So dissonance arises at first when some new information or knowledge is acquired which challenges some essential part of the original structure.

Not all new information is inconsistent. Much can be absorbed without disturbing the system or the group. Dissonance occurs only when there is a radical lack of fit; if one element implies the direct negative of another. 'To put it in more formal terms x and y are dissonant if not-x follows from y' (p. 88). It is not hard to construct theoretical examples; Carroll offers several (pp. 88, 90–93), so let one suffice here. Suppose you believe that the power of the gospel is irresistible, that anyone who hears it is bound to recognize its truth. After some time you acquire the information, verified by many reliable reports and by personal experience, that numerous people are entirely unmoved when they hear the gospel, and indeed reject it out of hand. The new knowledge is a clear disconfirmation of the original belief, and is likely to create dissonance. Suppose also that you believe that acceptance of the gospel is necessary for salvation, and that all mankind will ultimately be saved. The inconsistencies involved are now very strong, and may well produce an intolerable dissonance. We will now consider how this dissonance can be handled, and the conditions under which it can be reduced or avoided.

There are, according to Carroll, three important elements in the response to dissonance. They are 'explanatory or rationalizing schemes, the avoidance of sources of dissonance arousal and the centrality of the social group' (p. 93). In the example above the subject might (a) use some explanatory device such as, 'They may *appear* not to have accepted the truth, but in the end, perhaps on their death-bed, they will believe', or (b) refuse to accept the evidence, or even more likely, simply ignore it, as long as a sufficiently powerful distraction (such as getting on with the evangelistic work) is available, or (c) take refuge in the social group to which he or she belongs, and use that community as a defence against hostile information. This last is perhaps the best means of reducing dissonance, precisely because it is in a group where the individual feels 'at home' that the most powerful reinforcement of cognitions will be available to counter dissonance-producing information. Carroll is worth quoting at some length here:

> The majority of methods for reducing dissonance are to be found in this category of social support. If the main point in dissonance resolution is to reduce the force of the dissonant cognitions this may be achieved by the group. In the first place the existence of the group provides social validation for its beliefs — it is a confirming instance of the group's holdings. Additional cognitive elements, i.e. more people joining the group, may be added to the group thereby increasing the power base of its cognitions. If more and more people come to share the group's cognitive beliefs then (it is argued) there must be something right or influential about those beliefs. Commitment to a group followed by schemes for converting others to that group are probably the most effective social methods of resolving dissonance. (p. 95)

Festinger[5] has set out the conditions under which 'we would expect to observe increased fervour following the disconfirmation of a belief':

There are five such conditions.

1. A belief must be held with deep conviction and it must have some relevance to action, that is, to what the believer does or how he behaves.

2. The person holding the belief must have committed himself to it; that is, for the sake of his belief, he must have taken some important action that is difficult to undo. In general, the more important such actions are, and the more difficult they are to undo, the greater is the individual's commitment to the belief.

3. The belief must be sufficiently specific and sufficiently concerned with the real world so that events may unequivocally refute the belief.

4. Such undeniable disconfirmatory evidence must occur and must be recognized by the individual holding the belief.

5. The individual believer must have social support. It is unlikely that one isolated believer could withstand the kind of disconfirming evidence we have specified. If, however, the believer is a member of a group of convinced persons who can support one another, we would expect the belief to be maintained and the believers to attempt to proselyte (*sic*) or to persuade non-members that the belief is correct.

Before moving on to the application I wish to make, some reservations are in order. Cognitive dissonance theory is not appealed to here as a kind of magical solution to the dilemmas which attend the meeting of religions. It is used simply as a handy descriptive tool for setting out what seem to me to be the essential features of the problem: it reveals rather than explains. Its importance lies in its being drawn from experience outside the sphere of religious commitment, thus providing an opportunity to lower the temperature to a level which will permit a reasonably cool and dispassionate view of what can often be a highly controversial subject. But like all general theories it is something of a blunt instrument, capable of attracting attention, but without the subtlety necessary for fine analysis.

Besides this general caveat, there are a number of particular points that should be borne in mind. Thus, though the theory demands a situation in which two mutually inconsistent cognitions are simultaneously present, the required implication (that dissonance is thereby produced) may not always follow. People are in fact capable of absorbing surprising amounts of inconsistent evidence without even being aware of any conflict. Perhaps subconscious mechanisms are at work; repressions may be set up which will be a source of trouble in the long term; but in the short term, like the White Queen, many people are perfectly capable of believing as many as six impossible things before breakfast. Further, mere *logical* inconsistency is not perceived by the majority as being of existential significance; the definition of dissonant terms set out formally above ('x and y are dissonant if not-x follows from y') is fine for mathematicians and the like, but really rather remote from the terms of reference of a believer, or group of believers. So when we are looking for conflicting cognitions, it will be necessary to ensure that the *subjects* perceive them as being in conflict, not that they are *theoretically* inconsistent.

Festinger's conditions (1) and (2) place great stress on the importance of convictions with practical implications, and commitment to these convictions expressed in the form of practical action. In certain narrowly-defined circumstances this is relatively straightforward. Thus in the case described by Festinger and his co-authors in *When Prophecy Fails*, we have a specific prediction (of a great flood on 21 December) demanding belief, and practical implications (such as giving up one's job, enduring ridicule) the fulfilment of which testify to depth of commitment. But even here it is not always possible to list clear external criteria. Some of those involved were students, for whom commitment did not entail more than a temporary inattention to studies: must their commitment therefore be deemed less 'deep'? It may be, of course, that the theory is only applicable where objective criteria for the measurement of commitment are available; on the other hand, deeply held convictions do not always issue in immediately obvious practical consequences, but are none the less deeply held. Those who are passionately convinced of the efficacy of judicial execution for the crime of murder, for example, are rarely in a position (one would hope) to take any practical action as a result. Yet the consequences of any decisive proof of the uselessness of capital punishment would, I suspect, produce a powerful dissonance. The limitations demanded by Festinger's five conditions are undoubtedly wise, particularly if the theory is to be applied to or tested in a practical case. And the danger of sitting too lightly to these limitations is that we may end up with a philosophical rather than sociological expression of the original psychological theory. The application I wish to make is perhaps open to this danger, but is I believe still worth making.

Festinger's example relates to specific predictions and their failure to materialize. His theory speaks of beliefs – and does not explicitly state that these must be in the form of predictions. There does not seem to be any compelling reason why this restriction should have to apply, though it certainly produces examples of a sharply defined nature which are (presumably) limited in duration. Beliefs of other kinds can certainly satisfy the condition that they be capable of refutation. Thus for many centuries it was widely believed that the earth was flat – a belief whose religious overtones are revealed by the fact that, five hundred years after it was disconfirmed by Columbus's failure to fall over the edge of the world, it still has adherents who seek to convince the rest of us of the error of our perceptions (and the dangers of transatlantic travel!) Can cognitive dissonance be usefully applied to such circumstances? More seriously, can we apply it to circumstances where a long-established belief of a respectable kind, held by a great many people, is subjected to effective disconfirmation which gradually penetrates the group-awareness? I believe that we can, though cautiously, and strictly as a means of describing the mechanisms at work.

One other modification noted by Carroll[6] is that the group which has suffered dissonance will only seek to make new converts, as a response to dissonance, if it has 'minimal social support' and is 'subject to ridicule by outsiders'. 'Where there was solid social support and a friendly environment there was little evidence of any conversionist programme.' This seems obvious enough. Tension is clearly reduced in a friendly milieu. Yet even this can be overtly tampered with as a result of dissonance. Sometimes a group will seek to create or will imagine a hostile response where none (or very little) exists, thus supplying by their own efforts the missing condition! Examples can be found amongst fundamentalist and conservative groups within Christianity. Fundamentalist groups characteristically hold beliefs in the infallibility of scripture and the scientific accuracy of the biblical creation narratives which cannot be reconciled with the general literary and scientific consensus. These beliefs have practical consequences (conformity to group norms, avoidance of unlawful doubts and questions, refusal of social intercourse with out-groups) which are severely restricting and hard to justify if the beliefs are refuted. Disconfirmation undoubtedly exists: as far as any scientific matter can be settled, the Bible's view of creation is wholly incorrect, and literary and textual studies leave no room for doubt that the biblical text we have is fallible. The classic responses to dissonance are certainly present: rationalization ('creationism' is presented as a pseudo-science, the infallibility of the 'original autograph' of the Bible is asserted); avoidance – 'I cannot see any errors in the Bible'; and group solidarity along with a highly developed sense of betrayal when any member of the group strays from the accepted norm. Yet in the modern world there is little serious opposition to conservative views. Some intellectuals and academics may protest against what they see as deliberate obscurantism,[7] but in fact the general position of conservative Christianity, if not fundamentalism, is rather well-received by wide sections of the community. It presents itself as defending traditional morality, and as representing the simple man's understanding of the simple gospel in the face of 'pedantic scholarship', tactics which lend it ready acceptance. Conservative Christian groups have had considerable influence on political developments both in the USA and in Britain in recent years, for the mood of political conservatism which dominates both countries at present is very much in tune with their religious conservatism. Despite all this, there is a constant stream of complaint from evangelical religious circles that they are victims of discrimination, attack by alliances of 'liberals', and persecution because of their beliefs. They present, in short, a form of group paranoia, expressed as a belief in the conspiracy theory of the universe. My point is this: that, experiencing real feelings of dissonance because of the misfit described above, they have been forced to invent a hostile environment in order to justify a militantly proselytizing stance in a situation which, under the simpler analysis, would not require it. And there is certainly no doubt that it is the conservative and fundamentalist groups which most actively seek converts. They have brought to a fine art the process of conviction by numbers: they are forever counting heads – 3,000 at this rally, 10,000 at that, 15,000 converts from a Luis Palau campaign. That the claim to be attracting such large numbers directly contradicts the belief that the world is against them seems hardly to be noticed: this is one potential dissonance that doesn't get off the ground!

– 3 –

Festinger applied cognitive dissonance to a group looking for the imminent fulfilment of a specific prediction – a group, moreover of a very marginal and eccentric kind. Carroll used it as a hermeneutic[8] tool for interpreting certain aspects of Old Testament prophecy. Both of these are somewhat remote from contemporary life and thought, though both are instructive in their own way for more general situations. What I hope to do is to make an application of the theory to the dilemma described in the first section of this chapter in order to show why dialogue, which may from certain aspects look like a most rational and reasonable solution to the problem of what to do about mission, is in fact regarded from within the church with considerable suspicion, and is indeed actively opposed in some circumstances.

1. The modern missionary movement without doubt inspired deep conviction in very many people, a conviction that had a very strong relevance to action. It is not possible to take the call to mission seriously and do nothing about it, for the very terms in which the call is expressed (characteristically in Matthew 28) demand a response.

2. Commitment to the call to mission is seen in various ways. The first and most obvious is that of individuals who engage themselves through a church or society to be missionaries in some other country. Secondly, churches and mission societies, as organizations, have usually invested extensive funds, manpower, and equipment in the task of sending out missionaries. Thirdly, numbers of men and women who may never formally become 'missionaries' devote their time, energy and resources to supporting 'the cause'. And finally, the conviction that Christianity, as the one true faith, is called upon to assert its truth over against all other forms of belief is widely and firmly held by a great many individual Christians, and by nearly all churches and sects. This may not entail any direct practical action, but it frequently represents an intellectual and emotional investment the negation of which would be seriously life-threatening. That this is so can be seen from two comments, made in response to such a challenge, by one of those involved in the interfaith seminar described in Chapter 7:[9]

> This kind of view renders worthless all the missionary efforts of many centuries.
>
> The idea of anonymous Christians helps to reconcile the great commission in Matthew 28 with the apparent failure of mission in so many parts of the world.

The first of these gives expression to the dissonance experienced, but even as it does so denies it by using language which is intended to discredit the view which is felt to be dissonant. Thus we note here an example of coping with dissonance by avoidance: 'what you say is so unthinkable that it must be false'. This response was possible because the challenge came in the form of a theoretical opinion about Christianity's being just one of many faiths, and could therefore be directly denied. The second comment, however, is an example of rationalization. The challenge this time did not arise from the expression of an opinion, but was clearly seen to be implicit in certain accepted facts. Since the facts (that mission had been singularly ineffective in many places) could not be denied, the new theory of 'anonymous Christians'[10] was introduced to reduce dissonance. The ploy used here was particularly effective, for the new theory is in fact unfalsifiable. No conceivable factual information can be inconsistent with it, and so it can never produce dissonance.

3. The most important clause in the conditions for cognitive dissonance is that which insists on a belief being specific and rooted in the real world in such a way that unequivocal refutation is possible. This is actually a remarkably rare circumstance, for human beings are almost boundlessly ingenious when it comes to finding ways round the obstacle presented by strong arguments supported by hard evidence. In the volume *New Essays in Philosophical Theology* Antony Flew quotes what must be the classic example of dissonance avoidance by rationalization, the so-called 'Parable of the Gardener' (first developed by John Wisdom):[11]

Once upon a time two explorers came upon a clearing in the jungle. In the clearing were growing many flowers and many weeds. One explorer says, 'Some gardener must tend this plot'. The other disagrees. 'There is no gardener.' So they pitch their tents and set a watch. No gardener is ever seen. 'But perhaps he is an invisible gardener.' So they set up a barbed-wire fence. They electrify it. They patrol with bloodhounds. . . . But no shrieks ever suggest that some intruder has received a shock. No movements of the wire ever betray an invisible climber. The bloodhounds never give cry. Yet still the Believer is not convinced. 'But there is a gardener, invisible, intangible, insensible to electric shocks, a gardener who has no scent and makes no sound, a gardener who comes secretly to look after the garden which he loves.' At last the Sceptic despairs, 'But what remains of your original assertion? Just how does what you call an invisible, intangible, eternally elusive gardener differ from an imaginary gardener or even from no gardener at all?'

We cannot prevent the operation of this mechanism, though we can certainly hope that when it is taken *ad absurdum* those of a more reasonable turn of mind will recognize it for what it is. What we *may* be able to do is to identify certain kinds of unfalsifiable belief as primarily responses to cognitive dissonance. The hypothesis about anonymous Christians would, I suggest, fall into that category.

For the purposes of satisfying Festinger's conditions, however, let me propose the following as refutable beliefs bound up with the missionary movement:

(a) The message of Christianity is universal and its truth will be recognized by all people.

(b) The power of the gospel as mediated by God's Holy Spirit is irresistible.

(c) The gospel is the only means of salvation, and all will at the last be saved.

I include (c) because, though not a normative belief, it nonetheless occurs as a persistent conviction amongst a significant minority of evangelical Christians – and is indeed one of the more attractive elements in the missionary movement.

4. It seems to me to be obvious that both (a) and (b) have been comprehensively refuted by the known facts. A great many people have found the message of Christianity to be limited, hopelessly compromised by Western values, and discredited by its own history. Its truth is far from being recognized by any more than a minority of the people of the world. Thus we must conclude that (a) is false. As for (b), the heroic efforts of the last century and a half (not to mention the great missionary expansion of the church in earlier centuries) have signally failed to produce much evidence that the gospel is irresistible. Rather we now have quite strong evidence that people who already hold strong beliefs easily resist the appeal of Christianity. (b) therefore, is also false. The same evidence which serves to refute (a) and (b) must automatically disconfirm (c). Indeed this last belief is the weakest of the three, and the one most likely to fail. It is also, as it happens, the one whose disconfirmation tends to be readily accepted. Since it is a complex of two cognitions, it is theoretically possible for dissonance to be resolved by rejecting either one of the two. Some may retreat to a hardline position – only through Christianity can anyone find salvation; more likely is the alternative, that salvation will come to be seen as a valid aspect of various different faiths in their different ways. I say that this is more likely because anyone who has felt (c) to be a true cognition is already disposed to a universalist understanding of God's love, and is therefore psychologically prepared to go the step further which abandonding the first condition entails.

5. Social support. There is undoubtedly a well developed structure of support for those who maintain such views as (*a*) and (*b*). Missionaries who are on leave from 'the mission field' are expected to give a series of talks which will avoid awkward or threatening questions, and will reinforce the home supporters in their conviction that the work progresses satisfactorily, and that (in one small corner at least) the word of God is advancing as expected. In return for this endorsement of the traditional beliefs, those who actually work with unbelievers in distant parts are fêted and praised, so that the memory of the community's trust and gratitude stays with them in those moments of doubt when it is not quite so easy to believe that the great advance of the gospel is being maintained. What we have then is a doubly reinforcing system: each partner in the cause *must* encourage the other; for to raise any doubts, on either side, is nothing short of betrayal. Those at home *need* (like an addict needs a drug) periodic infusions of good news from the field; and their awareness of the vulnerability of the people they have sent out prevents them from saying or doing anything that might seem like a betrayal of trust. And on the other hand, those who have committed their lives to missionary work need constant reassurance that their work has meaning, and so are predisposed to make much of very little ('Faithful Ahmad learned another verse of the Swahili New Testament today! Praise the Lord!'). Further, since they are materially supported by gifts from home (sometimes made at some cost to the giver), to make any serious criticism would be both ungracious and unwise.

– 4 –

Do we have a genuine cognitive dissonance pattern here? I think that we do, as I have tried to establish in section 3. If I can attempt a summary: the missionary movement held the belief that the gospel would carry all before it; that belief was backed up by the serious practical commitment of a great many groups and individuals; it has been effectively refuted; and there is strong social support for those who maintain the belief. What results or consequences can be detected?

(*a*) Proselytism. It is rather striking that there has been in recent years a noticeable upsurge in proselytism *in the traditionally Christian countries* by evangelical groups which are by nature strongly committed to the missionary imperative. We find that just when the missionary movement has gone into decline there are determined and repeated attempts to evangelize in the 'old'

Christian areas. It is, I think, plausible to suggest that this phenomenon is a characteristic response (and quite a successful one) to the dissonance introduced by the factors described in section 3 (4).

(b) Antagonism. Many who belong to the church, but who are outside the circles of conservative evangelicalism, find that it is increasingly difficult to establish any kind of relationships across that divide. Indeed, it is much easier to form common bonds with believers in other faiths than it is to penetrate the defensive wall behind which fundamentalism hides. And the more those outside try to be friendly, the more they are regarded with suspicion and carefully excluded. Conversations across the barrier are now well-nigh impossible, such is the strictness of the doctrinal position insisted upon by conservative groups. All of this is part of the general phenomenon I described at the end of section 2: the creation of an atmosphere of hostility in the face of a determinedly friendly world. We must have martyrs! And if the world won't oblige us with persecution, we'll make them for ourselves! I believe that this is a secondary reaction to dissonance, unconsciously developed to afford the necessary grounds for a militant campaign of proselytism.

(c) Offensive. The natural corollary to antagonism and proselytism is to go on the offensive. It is not enough to defend the walls and to win converts. Those outside who pose a threat must be attacked and discredited. Now it must at once be said that this stage is only reached by the extreme minority. Unfortunately, that minority sometimes finds itself in a position of real influence. In Northern Ireland, for example, extreme Protestantism, insofar as it can be described as religious, is militantly hostile to any group or individual it sees as being too liberal. And in the conditions prevailing in Ulster, such people have a significant voice in matters of importance. Similar groups in other parts of the UK rarely wield any effective power, because they are not perceived by the uncommitted majority as having any relevance. In the USA, on the other hand, the 'twice-born' and 'moral majority' have become a political force to be reckoned with, even although it is doubtful if more than a small minority of Americans in fact subscribe to the beliefs of these sects.

Outside the political sphere, a steady stream of books, films, magazines, pamphlets, video material and articles keeps the faithful informed and brings the conservative cause to the forefront. And it must be admitted that this is a battle which has been effectively won. The simplicity of the arguments, the financial resources available to present them, and the attractiveness of colourful and easily assimilated material which makes no intellectual demands – all this adds up to a considerable armoury with which to challenge the seeming evasiveness and caginess of those who refuse the black and white alternative in the interests of a more rounded and satisfying understanding of Christianity and its meaning for the world today. We are back where we started at the beginning of this chapter, with 'either/or' questions. 'Either the Bible is right or it is wrong.' 'Either Jesus is God or he was mad.' 'You either accept the gospel or you go to hell.' If we answer these questions we condemn ourselves. Equally, if we refuse to answer them we stand discredited and will in all probability find ourselves damned in the words of the letter to the Laodiceans in Revelation 3.15–16:

> I know your works: you are neither cold nor hot. Would that you were cold or hot! So, because you are neither cold nor hot, I will spew you out of my mouth.

There is only *one* way to counter this Catch 22. We must denounce the whole mode of questioning by means of simplistic alternatives as a perversion of truth and a denial of the Bible's own teaching. Scripture does not set out a series of black and white alternatives. It offers a whole range of possibilities from which we may select, under whatever guidance we recognize, those that speak to us and to our situation in the world. Hermeneutic, in short, is also dialogue.

(d) This brings me to one last response. So far we have examined ways in which the dissonance experienced can be dealt with through reinforcement of the beliefs and the community under threat. A possibility not yet considered is that the disconfirming evidence be accepted and some alternative to the discredited belief sought. Dialogue is one attempt to find such an alternative. It sets to one side, if not wholly rejecting, the idea that the approach to other faiths should be through mission. It admits that some kind of equal standing must be allowed to all believers of whatever persuasion. And it is resolute in refusing to proselytize. Obviously it must therefore come into direct conflict with the responses in (a)–(c); and because these are strong responses to dissonance, the antagonism roused by dialogue will often be quite fierce. If those who advocate dialogue are right, then all that is represented by (a), (b), and (c) is under fresh challenge. Thus dialogue itself is seen as a cognition which is inconsistent with the very system that developed as a response to a disconfirming cognition! To choose dialogue rather than mission is regarded as defeatism, a surrender to the enemy. Even those who favour dialogue will often insist that they still expect conversions: we noted this, for example, in our discussion of Lesslie Newbigin's essays.[12]

We ought to recognize that dialogue is a radical transformation of part of the essential nature of Christianity. Perhaps it is too radical – though I doubt that. The shape of Christianity has undergone some very dramatic changes in the last two thousand years, and it would be a bold individual who dared to say that no more change was needed. If, as the reformers claimed, the church is *semper reformanda* there is no reason whatever to suppose that the process has ended. It could be that the church of the future will be a church in dialogue: the vision, at any rate, is not an ignoble one.

– 5 –

The delicacy of the whole question can be illustrated by one practical case. In Chapter 6 I described the Sharing of Faiths movement in Glasgow. It will be recalled that while there is strictly no attempt at proselytizing on the part of any one of the faiths involved, neither is there any question of blurring the distinctions between them. Muslims remain decidedly Muslim, Jews do not cease to be Jews, Hindus and Christians are true to their own convictions. What is aimed at is an increase of understanding and a certain degree of sharing (deliberately left undefined). In fact, no formal dialogue takes place, so what happens is at least one stage removed from the situation envisaged in the preceding discussion.

Despite this, there has consistently been opposition from Christian quarters to Sharing of Faiths. From time to time unhappiness has been expressed that no evangelizing is done, and the work of the International Flat has been criticized by those who feel that, since the finance for it comes from Christian organizations, some kind of dividend in the form of conversions ought to be forthcoming. No practical restrictions have resulted from these undercurrents, but if they were to become stronger the principle of 'he who pays the piper calls the tune' might one day come into effect.

One concrete example shows what can happen. It has been the practice of the Sharing of Faiths Committee to advertise its annual Presentation by means of a leaflet sent to all members of the Presbytery of Glasgow. This leaflet contains a summary of the

aims of the movement. The following appeared in the Reports to
the Presbytery, February 1983:

> The attention of Presbytery has been drawn to the allegedly
> syncretistic nature of the phrase 'the spiritual unity of all
> religion' appearing in the Presentation of Faiths leaflet which is
> sent out with the billet usually in the May posting. After
> consultation with the Convener of the Church and Community
> Committee it was agreed that the words 'the spiritual unity of all
> religion' should be re-placed with 'the universal religious aspir-
> ations of all mankind'. It is recommended that Presbytery ask
> that this alteration be made when the next leaflet is produced.
>
> (Definition: Syncretism is the mixture of various systems of
> thought.)

When the matter came before Presbytery, an Addendum was
moved and seconded:

> It is further recommended that Presbytery express its whole-
> hearted support for the continuing work of the Sharing of Faiths
> Committee, recognizing it as a unique forum where represen-
> tatives of six World Faiths can meet in mutual trust and spiritual
> brotherhood.

No decision was made: the whole matter (report and addendum)
was taken back to the Overseas Committee for further consideration. Finally, in May 1983, that committee presented the following
report to Presbytery:

> The Committee is unanimously agreed that the term 'Spiritual
> Brotherhood' retains an overtone of syncretism.

This was received by Presbytery with no further comment. In effect
what the Presbytery of Glasgow had done was to refuse to endorse,
as requested, the work of the Sharing of Faiths Committee, and to
make as its only response a somewhat pedantic remark about the
slightly syncretistic character of a particular phrase used in the
publicity leaflet.

One last instalment of the story should be recorded. The Sharing
of Faiths Committee has, since these events, adopted as part of the
definition of its aims the following statement:

> The Sharing of Faiths aims to create understanding between
> different communities and to express spiritual brotherhood
> across religious barriers.

It seems unlikely that Presbytery will be any more ready to accept this as a satisfactory definition. The offending term, 'spiritual brotherhood' is still used. It is in fact hard to see in what sense this is a denial of Christianity – perhaps the real offence lies in its suggestion that faith in all its diverse forms is something which transcends the artificial barriers of race, colour and religion. We should therefore see the opposition to it as a dissonance response arising from fear.

Curiously, no one (to my knowledge) has objected to the genuinely offensive aspect of the statement: the use of the term 'brotherhood'. But then the church is still sadly behind in its recognition of the barriers of sexism. There is a dialogue between men and women waiting to be done. And if we have experienced dissonance in the arena of interfaith relations, that is probably nothing to the culture shock which some sectors of the church have coming to them! Perhaps, when we can finally recognize the reality of the spiritual *community* of men and women of *all* faiths, we will be able to say that dialogue has truly begun. But I fear it will be a long time coming.

10

Dialectic

It may be that . . . we must understand faith not as *certainty* but as *creative tension*: a phrase which has been greatly devalued by overuse, but which is hard to improve upon as a suggestive description of the dialectical character of the interaction of faith with life and the means of revelation.[1]

– I –

It will be obvious that the intention of this study is to argue for an open and flexible style of faith which can be sensitive to 'the other' without compromising its own perceptions. There are dangers and temptations in such an approach. We may lose our identity in a sort of soup into which various half-understood beliefs have been thrown to give an exotic effect. The naive may be carried off into another religious realm for the wrong reasons – perhaps because they imagine, for example, that they can escape from all the crassness and materialism of Christianity by retreating to a Tibetan monastery in Eskdalemuir or an Ashram in India. And there is the temptation of syncretism, the mirage of a perfect faith formed by choosing all the nice bits from the world religions. Syncretism itself is not wrong – all faiths are to some degree amalgams of diverse systems. Christianity for instance is a blend of Judaism, Hellenism, and the Roman Imperium. And of course Christianity is by no means alone in this respect. By the first century CE Judaism had been strongly influenced by Hellenism, Persian mythology, and the traditional popular religion of Canaan. Islam is clearly indebted to both Judaism and Christianity. Sikhism has consciously combined elements of both Islam and Hinduism. And Hinduism itself is the great grandfather of all syncretistic faiths, and the one that proves my point most forcefully. It has absorbed just about every faith the world has ever known in one form or another, yet is still undeniably itself (though admittedly, that 'self' is notoriously hard to define)! What is important is not what these great faiths owe to each other and to their past: what gives them their force is the presence of a compelling guiding insight or revelation. Christianity is primarily to do with Christ; Islam is founded on the Qur'an; Judaism is identified by Torah and Talmud. But where syncretism is the whole matter, where we find nothing more than a well-intentioned homogenization of religion, it will fail. For one thing, the world we seek to understand is, sadly, very far from being well-intentioned. And for another, faith without a fire in the belly will never win converts. It is the Esperanto of the religious sphere, doomed from the start, and for very similar reasons.

Nevertheless, as long as we recognize the dangers we can take the open approach to other faiths. There is, though, a feedback phenomenon: thinking about our *own* faith can – indeed must – also have an aspect of openness to it. Otherwise we will find ourselves attempting an impossible intellectual feat: the openness of a dialogical relationship with other faiths combined with a rigid set of beliefs enshrining our own faith. It is for this reason that I want to return to the comment I made earlier (quoted at the head of this chapter) about the dialectical nature of faith, and explore it a little further. I want to suggest that within the fundamental and founding norm of belief in the person and teaching of Jesus there is remarkably wide scope for the kind of exploration and rediscovery of which Chapter 4 may serve as a particular example.

The dialectical model which we are familiar with from Marx (who used it to propound his philosophy of history) and which we probably wrongly associate with Hegel[2] affords a useful analytical tool. Without claiming any deep significance for it, I would still want to claim that the pattern of 'thesis-antithesis-synthesis becoming new thesis' provides an explanatory mode of wide applicability. Whether or not this is how history progresses (as the marxian analysis would hold) is unimportant for our purposes, which are much more limited. The model is, I believe, a helpful approximation to the way we advance our thinking in many spheres. Assuming we do not wish to maintain a fixed position, whenever new information or new ideas become available what we at first held as a 'thesis' is challenged by an 'antithesis' of a more or less radical nature. It is at this point that the relevance of the dialectical method becomes apparent; for it is quite rare for people in this position to adopt *either* hypothesis exclusively. What tends to happen is that thesis and antithesis interact to form a new hypothesis (the 'synthesis') on the basis of which the whole process starts again. Plainly this is a continuing dialogue or dialectic: it is inherently open-ended, there is a built-in mechanism which logically excludes the possibility of having the last word. Moreover it is important that dialectic itself should not come to be thought of as a rigid or pedantic affair. As Richard Kroner writes:

'Dialectic' originally meant 'conversation' or 'dialogue', and Hegel's dialectic, like Plato's, might be called 'the dialogue of mind with itself'. Logic, like thinking, moves from opposites to opposites, posing, opposing, composing the contents of thought, transforming them into ever new concepts or categories. But it is by no means the mere application of a monotonous trick that could be learned and repeated. It is not the mere imposition of an ever recurring pattern. It may appear so in the mind of some historians who catalogue the living trend of thought; but in reality it is an ever changing, ever growing development. Hegel is nowhere pedantic in pressing concepts into a ready-made mold. The theme of thesis, antithesis, and synthesis, like the motif of a musical composition, has many modulations and modifications.[3]

Bearing these things in mind let us venture some thoughts on faith as dialectic rather than dogma, in the hope that we may shed some light on the way that belief can operate in dialogue both with its own historic and contemporary roots, and with the insights and revelations of other systems.

— 2 —

A Dialectic of Faith

When Jesus said, or was reported as having said, 'Ask, and it will be given you; seek, and you will find; knock, and it will be opened to you', a thesis was established which has proved both attractive and enduring. Whatever its original context or intended application, it has been generally appropriated as a proof-text for a wide range of faith situations: answer to prayer, establishment of correct doctrine, removal of doubt, etc. It has served both as a promise (that answers or replies will be forthcoming) and as a challenge (to go on seeking even when no light can be discerned). It has probably been most potent when these two dimensions have acted in concert, offering a paradigm of faith travelling confidently knowing that the journey has an end which will be revealed. Distortions of the thesis include its use to defend closed positions ('We already have the answers') and naive misunderstandings of prayer ('All you have to do is ask'). But most thoughtful Christians would probably accept that these are indeed distortions, that whatever Jesus may have intended he did not offer easy answers or cheap intercessory prayer.

We might well be content with this thesis for most of our lives; certainly as long as things go reasonably smoothly and nothing occurs which our set of working hypotheses cannot cope with. But challenges can arise which call this whole structure in question. Particularly vulnerable is the belief that those who ask will be answered. Who, for example (apart from the Nazis) answered the Jews at Auschwitz? Were bullets all that the blacks at Sharpeville found in response to their search for justice? Where should we send all the anonymous individual victims of the world's perennial hunger, homelessness and disease to look for answers to their questions? Do we fully realize, those of us who are the material beneficiaries of the rich West, that every time we say the Lord's Prayer we take for granted an answer that millions are dying to hear? 'Give us this day our daily bread' is a cliche to us; to them it represents a cry of despair. Then again, which of us has listened to that anguished response to grief or tragedy, 'Why me, O Lord, why me?' without at least a silent recognition that there are some questions which cannot be answered. Not that there is anything new in this. The prophets and psalmists of Israel gave voice to the same deep sense of despair in words that we still repeat; let one example suffice, whose significance will be at once apparent:

> My God, my God, why hast thou forsaken me?
> Why art thou so far from helping me,
>   from the words of my groaning?
> O my God, I cry by day, but thou dost not answer;
>   and by night, but find no rest (Ps. 22.1–2).

It ought to give us some food for thought that these words are found on Jesus' lips at the final crisis of his life (Matt. 27.46; Mark 15.34). Whether he actually uttered them hardly matters: what is significant is that they were thought to be appropriate by those who told the story and wrote down the gospel traditions. At the heart of the cross, it seems, there is an unanswered question.

There is when you think about it something fitting about that fact, for it reminds us that the scriptures which were Jesus' scriptures present a many-sided picture. From elation to despair, from simple faith to complex doubt, from the finest expressions of love to the most basic urge to vengeance, from the elaborate vanity of cultic ritual to the elemental call to justice, love and peace – all are to be found in these pages. So alongside our thesis: faith seeking understanding is true faith, must be placed the unanswered doubts of the psalmist, the despair of Job, and the seeming cynicism of Ecclesiastes. Here then are the terms of the antithesis, from these three ancient questioners:

(*a*) My God, my God, why hast thou forsaken me?

(*b*) Vanity of vanities, says the Preacher, vanity of vanities! All is vanity. When I applied my mind to know wisdom, and to see the business that is done on earth, how neither day nor night one's eyes see sleep; then I saw all the work of God, that man cannot find out the work that is done under the sun. However much man may toil in seeking, he will not find it out; even though a wise man claims to know, he cannot find it out. (Eccles. 1.2; 8.16–17)

(*c*)   Know then that God has put me in the wrong,
               and closed his net about me.
    Behold, I cry out 'Violence!' but I am not answered;
               I call aloud, but there is no justice.
    He has walled up my way, so that I cannot pass,
               and he has set darkness upon my paths. (Job 19.6–8)

These passages are by no means isolated examples; nor are they mere academic illustrations. Each in its own way represents the struggle of a human being with the terrible mystery of God's silence. The first comes from the context of a people's worship, from the liturgy and the prayers of the Jews down through the centuries. The second is a scholar's more resigned, but still engaged response: if we can say nothing, and if to speak of God is to be guilty of pride, perhaps cynicism (realism?) is the only 'answer'. The third comes to us as part of a great dramatic dialogue, in which Job and his several friends search (in vain, it seems) for *some* light on the dark subject of innocent suffering. Each of these has its counterpart in our own time, each still expresses for us what faith scarcely dares to put in words: the silence of God, the failure of the promise. We have sought – dear God how we have sought – but have not found. Thesis/antithesis. Belief/disconfirmation. Cognition/dissonance.

What then of synthesis? If faith seeks an answer, and silence is all, can we say (at the risk of seeming naive) that silence is the answer? Of course we cannot, at least, not in that too easy way. We are emphatically not to endorse the individual who says, God's 'no' is an answer too. 'You asked for the wrong thing, so God slapped you down, like a naughty child!' We are not discussing here petty matters like requests for sun on holiday or help to pass exams. What is at issue is the asking of questions of life and death, of the ultimate meaning of our existence, and of the nature of the God we wish we believed in. To take no for an answer is to demean both the question and the questioner, and so to diminish also That to which we put the question. There is however a way to make sense of the synthesis: we *will* not admit that silence is an answer; but we may accept that it is in silence that faith must now seek what answer is to be found.

The psalmist's cry of despair, 'My God, my God', expressed his anguish at being abandoned by the very God without whom existence had no meaning. But at least he had one thing going for him: it was from within a worshipping community that he uttered his soul-searching cry. He did not stand alone – a fact which both gave him strength and placed upon his unwilling shoulders an inescapable responsibility. In another place the poet, having voiced his resentment at the prosperity of the wicked (73.3–14), goes on to say:

> If I had said, 'I will speak thus',
>> I would have been untrue
>>> to the generation of thy children.
> But when I thought how to understand this,
>> it seemed to me a wearisome task,
>>> until I went into the sanctuary of God.
>>>> (vv. 15–17a)

There are two factors here which serve to lead the writer to another level of understanding faith. One is the sense of being part of a community of believers: it is as though ultimate surrender to doubt and despair is a betrayal not just of one's own faith, but of the faith of the whole community. 'If faith is pointless then it means that the whole tradition in which he has been nurtured is a fraud, and that the people with whom he worships and in whose company he seeks to serve God are wholly deluded. This conclusion he is not prepared to draw.'[4] This may or may not be an admirable attitude; in some ways it is like the group-reinforcement requirement of cognitive dissonance,[5] but it has a positive side to it represented by respect for and trust in the tradition and the community which embodies it. This is not the whole story, however. 'The sense of being upheld by the faith of the community . . . does not solve the psalmist's problem.' The second factor is the existence of a *place* where some kind of understanding, of acceptance can be found. 'It was in the temple, through some experience which came to him in worship, that the psalmist saw himself and his problem in a new light.' In the silence of the sanctuary there may still be found an awareness that the fussing and noise of our talk would otherwise block out.

The Preacher, on the other hand, teaches some kind of stoic resignation. You won't find answers, so stop asking, and make the best of what you have. It is not a particularly elevating message, and may well be seen as defeatist. But it is not necessarily an anti-religious attitude, and there are moments when his doctrine of cautious resignation is expressed in language which lifts it well above the realm of mere expediency. It was, after all, no dull pedant who wrote this:

> For everything there is a season,
>> and a time for every matter under heaven:
> a time to be born, and a time to die;
>> a time to plant, and a time to pluck up what is
>>> planted;
> a time to kill, and a time to heal;
>> a time to break down, and a time to build up;
> a time to weep, and a time to laugh;
>> a time to mourn and a time to dance;
>
>> ...
>
> a time to rend, and a time to sew;
>> a time to keep silence, and a time to speak;
> a time to love, and a time to hate;
>> a time for war, and a time for peace.
>
>> (Eccles. 3.1–4, 7–8)

And the pathos and despair of his description of the aging body's decline into impotence must place it amongst the most touching of laments on old age:

Take thought to your death[6] in the days of your youth, before the evil days come, and the years draw nigh, when you will say, 'I have no pleasure in them'; before the sun and the light and the moon and the stars are darkened and the clouds return after the rain; in the day when the keepers of the house tremble, and the strong men are bent, and the grinders cease because they are few, and those that look through the windows are dimmed, and the doors on the street are shut; when the sound of the grinding is low, and one rises up at the voice of a bird, and all the daughters of song are brought low; they are afraid also of what is high, and terrors are in the way; the almond tree blossoms, the grasshopper drags itself along and desire fails; because man goes to his eternal home, and the mourners go about the streets; before the silver cord is snapped, or the golden bowl is broken, or the pitcher is broken at the fountain, or the wheel broken at the cistern, and the dust returns to the earth as it was, and the spirit returns to God who gave it. Vanity of vanities, says the Preacher; all is vanity (Eccles. 12.1–8).

Whatever else we may say about the Preacher, there is one thing certain: he was not afraid to look upon the tragic mask. His theology may be minimal; but unlike many more wordy systems it embraces the fears of mankind as well as the hopes and does not belittle or disparage those radical doubts which, millennia later, Paul Tillich was to face again in his *The Courage to Be*. The writer of Ecclesiastes found no answers. It is doubtful if he would have expected to find any. But, having faced the failure of the thesis 'Seek and Find' he could still recommend living, not for answers, but for life itself, the great and only gift we have from God. 'In the day of prosperity be joyful, and in the day of adversity consider; God has made the one as well as the other, so that man may not find out anything that will be after him' (6.14). 'God is in heaven, and you upon earth; therefore let your words be few' (5.2b).

Job, who represents our third antithesis, is the finest example in the ancient world of an individual's lonely fight with the soul-destroying effects of unjust suffering. Where the psalmist spoke within and for the faithful community, Job speaks as one who is outcast, whose very suffering is taken to be proof of his rejection by God and society alike. He is the very epitome of noble endurance, even taken by some to be a prefiguration of Christ. Yet a close reading of the book as a whole produces a disturbing effect: Job's complaints become wearisome after a time. His constantly reiterated protestations of innocence, touching at first, gradually begin to nag at the reader like a decaying tooth and we find ourselves more in sympathy with the 'friends' than would have seemed possible at first. This increasing disenchantment is an important part of the drama. It is an example – perhaps the first? – of what McLuhan gave expression to in his memorable slogan, 'the medium is the message'. The alienation of the reader from Job and his problems is part of the message of that troublesome book. He is *utterly* alone. Not even posterity has sympathy with him. In 19.23–25 he gives voice to a prayer which has become one of the most memorable passages in the whole book:

Oh that my words were written!
Oh that they were inscribed in a book!

Oh that with an iron pen and lead
> they were graven in the rock for ever!
For I know that my Redeemer lives,
> and at last he will stand upon the earth.

The first part of this prayer, though literally fulfilled, is by a dark
dramatic irony negated by the effect his words have on those to
whom he appeals for vindication. And the second part of the prayer is
in Hebrew which has become so damaged and distorted that it is
virtually impossible to know what its original meaning was.[7] Thus
Job is twice silenced, once because we understand his words, and
again because we can no longer understand his words. Christian
piety has been content to see in the mysterious 'redeemer' (Hebrew
go'el) a prophecy of Christ; but this is unsubstantiated by the text
which belongs, insofar as it can be reconstructed, to the domain of
the law (while the word *go'el* is used poetically of ransoming from
death, its major use is as a legal term). Job anticipates that if his
testimony is preserved and read, some counsel for the defence will
come forward to acquit him. But none such appears and from now on
it is clear that the gap between Job and his advisers is unbridgable, as
his complaints increase and his speech becomes increasingly fretful
(see in particular ch. 31). He is ultimately unlovable. Our hearts do
not warm to him and though he deserves our understanding, he fails
somehow to win our sympathy.

Now this is a man who has without any shadow of a doubt pursued
the injunction to 'ask, seek, knock' with unremitting ardour. He has
asked and asked, he has been grossly importunate in his demands of
God. He has sought (as men seek for wisdom in ch. 28) high and low,
day and night. He has knocked and beat his fists against closed doors
until they bled with pain. But to no avail. His God remains resolutely
silent and hidden. His friends tell him to see sense. His wife offers
hard-headed advice: 'Do you still hold fast your integrity? Curse God
and die' (2.9). His modern readers (his latter-day 'friends') might find
it hard to believe that anyone could be quite so pure, and be inclined
rather to interpret his protestations as a sign of guilt than of innocence. Some have even analysed the dialogue as a record of psychological illness[8] – a peculiarly twentieth-century solution: whatever we
cannot stand or understand is labelled with one of the modern
synonyms for madness and locked away where it cannot touch
us.

We saw how the Preacher, with his sharp wit and (we may suppose)
no undue hardship to bear, found a meaning for life which encompassed the very elements which made meaning problematic. We discov-

ered that the Psalmist, bound up as he was with a believing
community, could find in the community the meaning and
purpose of his faith. But Job has alienated himself from all human
support, and his intellect serves only to demonstrate more forcibly
the vanity of his beliefs and the hopelessness of his case. Even in
such extremes, however, a dialogue can take place, and this is
what the final chapters of the book of Job are devoted to. At the
beginning of chapter 32, when Job's complaints have finally
ended, a new character enters the story. This man's name is *Elihu*,
and he speaks for six chapters – longer by far than any of the other
friends, half as long again as God himself, and equalled only by
Job's last set of speeches in chapters 26–31. There are a number of
important points to be noted:

(*a*) Elihu's name means 'He is my God', and it is quite clear that
'He' refers to Yahweh, the personal name of the God of Israel, and
the name used for God when he finally addresses Job in chapter
38.[9] Thus immediately we find a significance in the name which
is not present in the case of the other three advisers.

(*b*) Although Job responds volubly to the criticisms of his other
advisers, culminating in the lengthy speech which ends in chapter
31, he makes no response to Elihu at all. Elihu has done what
hitherto seemed impossible: he has rendered Job speechless. It is
not without significance that only Yahweh himself is able to force
out of Job the admission that has no reply to make (40.3–5; 42.1–
6).

(*c*) There are a number of features of Elihu's speech which
foreshadow the arguments to be used by Yahweh. (*i*) He appeals to
the character of God as creator and sustainer of the created order,
as the all-powerful at whose word the most unruly elements are
obedient (36.24–37.13). (*ii*) His manner of hurling unanswerable
questions at Job (e.g. 37.14–20) is exactly mirrored in God's
speeches (cf. ch. 38). (*iii*) The direct challenge to Job, who up until
now has been asking all the questions, is that he should answer –
if he can! (33.5, compare Yahweh's challenge in 38.1–3 and 40.1–
2).

Following immediately upon Elihu's exhortations, with no
word of reply from Job, no opportunity indeed for any reply, the
drama concludes with the speeches of Yahweh in person, 'out of
the whirlwind'. The language used here is designed to convey the
awesome and terrifying aspect of the presence of the Almighty,
whom to see is death, whose least word causes the whole earth to
shake to its very foundations. At the end of his first speech,
Yahweh gives Job an opportunity to speak (40.1–2):

And the Lord said to Job:
'Shall a faultfinder contend with the Almighty?
He who argues with God, let him answer it.'

At last! This is what Job has asked for: 'I would speak to the Almighty, and I desire to argue my case with God. . . . Behold, I have prepared my case; I know that I shall be vindicated. . . . Call, and I will answer; or let me speak, and do thou reply to me' (13.3, 18, 22). But here is a strange thing: this great man of words, this furious debater, has become strangely tongue-tied (40.3–5):

> Job answered the Lord:
> 'Behold, I am of small account;
>   what shall I answer thee?
> I lay my hand on my mouth.
> I have spoken once, and I will not answer;
>   twice, but I will proceed no further.'

Still this is not the end. Yahweh goes on to illustrate his power in the figures of the two great monsters Behemoth and Leviathan (40.15–41.34), a passage which has produced more than a little disagreement amongst interpreters. Some want to 'demythologize' the two beasts by identifying them as the hippopotamus and the crocodile respectively. This seems to me to misunderstand both the theology and the poetry of the passage. Surely the point is that Behemoth and Leviathan should be creatures which man could *never* conceivably master, creatures from the primordial nightmares of the human race and therefore a vivid expression of the mythical powers of raw untamed nature. It is in his control of them that God makes dramatically clear his absolute dominion over creation.

Having thus convincingly asserted his unique claims, Yahweh holds his peace. Now at last Job finds his voice. No longer does he argue and fume and fret. Yet there is more than just the somewhat sullen response of chapter 40, which might have been expressed in colloquial language as 'What's the point of saying anything? I've obviously said too much already, and I'd best keep my mouth shut from now on.' In his final confession he admits God's two specific charges against him ('Who is this that hides counsel . . . ' and 'Hear, and I will speak . . . ') and fights through to the realization that his mourning and his self-abasement have been an indulgence of self-pity rather than noble suffering: 'I despise myself, and repent of[10] dust and ashes.' Far from being a portrayal of a chastened and humiliated man, we have here something more like a shout of praise as the dark begins to lift and the light dawns (42.1–6):

> At last Job answered Yahweh:
> I know that you have power to do anything,
>   that nothing you intend can be thwarted.
> ['Who is this who hides wise advice without knowledge'
>   (cf. 38.2)]
> Therefore I declare! – though I do not understand;
>   wonders far beyond me! – though I do not comprehend.
> ['Listen, and I will speak;
>   I will question you, and you will explain to me'
>   (cf. 38.3)]
> I knew of you by hearsay,
>   but now I really see:
> Therefore I abandon my complaints,
>   ˙ and repent of dust and ashes!'

It was no easy answer that Job found, though if he had *begun* with that sort of statement we might justifiably have found him guilty of superficiality. It was only after he had gone through all the process of grief and protest, of wild railing against the fates, that the healing mechanism could begin. The book presents it as an external debate, though we might in modern terms express it as an inner dialogue. First Elihu, a human figure who clearly stands *in loco dei*, prepares Job for the inevitable: it is as if Job has for the first time become aware of issues beyond his own immediate circumstances. The voice of conscience, perhaps, has found personification in Elihu. Fittingly, the hero is silent at this juncture; words would be premature, and protest is past. Then comes the revelation, the gradual dawning of insight. That the process is a slow, reluctant one is demonstrated by Job's first response in 40.3–5. We do not abandon cherished beliefs lightly; and even if the final 'conversion' seems sudden, it only marks the last small step in what has been a long and eventful journey. So for Job the journey ends as we have seen with a new hope: the answers may never be found, but God remains, and with that realization there comes a kind of peace – *shalom* – that no 'outrageous fortune' can disturb. Until, of course, some new antithesis is born. For satisfying though this conclusion may be in artistic terms, the book of Job does not end there. It sums things up in a narrative passage which in a way makes a nonsense of the preceding drama, for it reverts to the old dogma that righteousness can be measured by prosperity: the very doctrine that Job had sweated blood to deny! 'The Lord restored the fortunes of Job, when he had prayed for his friends; and the Lord gave Job twice as much as he had before' (42.10). The process of dialectic is never still. Just when we think we've won through to a satisfactory understanding, another move is made, and faith is once again searching, restless as ever.

– 3 –

These new theses worked out by the Psalmist, the Preacher and Job are, of course, not the last word. They are themselves starting points. It will not have escaped the notice of alert readers that most of what I have so far said under the heading of 'A Dialectic of Faith' has been drawn from Old Testament examples. Now there is undoubtedly, on a large canvas, a dialectic between Old and New Testaments. At many points the New develops and reinterprets theological insights which first come to our attention in the Old. We have noted, for instance, how a work like Revelation uses the apocalyptic mode of certain Old Testament passages; and we have seen the importance of the intellectual tradition in Israel and its thoughts on the nature of 'wisdom' and 'word of God' for a fuller understanding of the theology of the prologue to John's Gospel. Can we identify a similar dialectic relating to the themes we have analysed at some length in the present chapter?

The central concern of the dialectic we have so far considered is the issue of innocent suffering. It would not, I think, be an exaggeration to say that any effective theology must offer a genuine solution to this problem – that is to say, it must deal with it seriously and not resort to quibbles to circumvent the question. The various strands that go to make up the New Testament represent a wide variety of engagements with this great mystery; their very multiplicity testifies both to the deep seriousness of the question and the fact that Christianity too is a faith in dialogue, always challenged to remember that a belief which becomes a dogma is like a prisoner's chain. Rather than attempt a full-scale discussion of New Testament theology, it seems appropriate at this juncture merely to indicate the lines along which the dialectic has proceeded in the early Christian period.

(a) If the great unanswered question of Job was 'How can a God who is just permit the suffering of a righteous person?', surely the most striking new move in Christianity was the revolutionary concept of *incarnation*. God himself, by a mystery we cannot comprehend, is identified with the suffering of his creation. Dare we say (with the mystics) that God himself suffers? Certainly Jesus, who represents or symbolizes this aspect of deity, drinks to the dregs the cup of suffering, and in speaking the words of the Psalm, 'My God, my God, why hast thou forsaken me?' takes to himself the anguished questions of tormented souls down the ages. Thus, in a way that the original writer can never have imagined, the confession of Psalm 139.7–12 finds fulfilment:

> Whither shall I go from thy Spirit?
> 	Or whither shall I flee from thy presence?
> If I ascend to heaven, thou art there!
> 	If I make my bed in Sheol, thou art there!
> If I take the wings of the morning
> 	and dwell in the uttermost parts of the sea,
> even there thy hand shall lead me,
> 	and thy right hand shall hold me.
> If I say, 'Let only darkness cover me,
> 	and let the light about me be night,'
> even the darkness is not dark to thee,
> 	the night is as bright as the day;
> 	for darkness is as light with thee.

(b) The encounter with Hellenistic and Persian religions and philosophies in the late pre-Christian era greatly influenced the direction taken by both Judaism and Christianity. Perhaps the most striking contribution from the latter source was the dualistic solution to the problem of good, evil and suffering. Although officially both religions deny this principle, it undoubtedly informs important areas in each case. Judaism's extreme reluctance to mention even indirectly the name of God led to something close to a deification of certain of his qualities or attributes. In gnosticism this was elaborated to a whole string of emanations of increasing remoteness from the God which culminated in a radically dualistic division between Creator and creation. Kabbalistic mysticism in medieval Judaism displays a number of similar characteristics, though it avoids the extremes of gnosticism. In Christian thinking a direct input from Zoroastrian mythology, most strikingly in the apocalyptic drama of Revelation, led to Satan and God being opposed for all practical purposes as equal powers fighting for control of the world and the souls of men and women. No doubt orthodox theology was always careful to preserve the supremacy of God, but popular faith very readily saw Satan as the source of all evil and unjust suffering, and so was able to exonerate God, thus solving (literally with a *deus ex machina*!) the whole problem. The fact that the absolute supremacy of God cannot be logically reconciled with the total responsibility of the Devil for all evil has rarely troubled popular expressions of Christian mythology; but it surely means that this approach is a retrograde step when compared with the honest struggles of Job and the Psalmists for understanding.

(c) There is one move originating in apocalyptic Jewish thinking and taken up by Christianity, which easily cuts the gordian knot of suffering – some would say too easily. God is just, we believe, and so all injustice will be put right. It is clear that this final settlement is not made in this life. Therefore it must be a function of the afterlife: on the day of judgment there will be a great reckoning, and all those who prospered in life will suffer in eternity, while the innocent poor will become great in the kingdom of heaven. It is undoubtedly true that this belief (or hope) is encouraged in the New Testament, and strongly motivated the life and actions of many early Christians. To an extent the doctrine of atonement, which interprets Jesus as God's agent in rescuing us from the inevitable consequences of sin, is tied up with this conviction. Like dualism, however, it somewhat cheapens the issue, for it essentially takes us back to the point of view against which Job protested so strenuously, that righteousness is rewarded and sin punished in some tangible and visible fashion. The concept of a just God who can consign some human beings to eternal perdition and others to eternal bliss when it is simultaneously agreed that 'all alike have sinned' is morally no better than that of a just God who permits the innocent suffering of his people. And at least there is some hope that in that suffering some sort of meaning may be found. I for one can find no coherent meaning in the theology of the day of judgment.

(d) Out of a variety of intellectual and religious traditions: the Preacher's remote but not unaware God, the concept of the creator God as one who calls the universe into being out of nothing (in contrast with the older idea of a God who imposes order on the primordial chaos), the stress on the importance of the word as an expression of *torah* (God's will and guidance), and the role given to wisdom as God's assistant at creation, there emerges in New Testament times the vision of the grand divine plan. The prologue to John's Gospel (1.1–18) is possibly the finest expression of it, but it appears in a number of different places and in different guises. It underlies the Pauline concept of election, and it informs his impassioned plea for the Jews in Romans 9–11. Its power lies in a very simple point: that no human mind can possibly understand more than a small part of God's grand design. Therefore, if we accept the principle that all is ordained and nothing lies outside his will, then we can rest content with what we may make sense of, leaving the rest either for later enlightenment, or for a full revelation in the world to come. 'For now we see in a mirror dimly, but then face to face. Now I know in part; then I shall understand fully, even as I have been fully understood' (I Cor. 13.12). While the notion of the grand design is a helpful metaphor, it will not stand close examination. It reduces human free will (if that is important) to the status of a legal fiction, and it supposes that the future is something like a videorecording being played back which is therefore predictable in detail, that it 'exists' before it happens. It is this idea which encourages the use of the Old Testament as a collection of detailed prophecies of the events both of Jesus' life and of the history of the church. Apart from the basic fallacy that all such interpretation depends upon hindsight, and (outside those meanings enshrined by New Testament convention) depends also on the beliefs and attitudes of the group making the interpretation, this procedure (were it successful) would reduce life to the meaningless performance of a prepared script, the only interest being that most of us are prevented from seeing the text in advance! Therefore, though there is undoubtedly some validity in the concept of the divine plan, we must not expect it to be reliable in all its details, and we must never use it as an escape hatch in the face of the genuine problems of life.

(e) I would like to add one last piece to this infinite jigsaw which we call faith. In appropriating the rhetoric of the suffering servant in Isaiah 40–55 and giving it concrete expression in terms of the suffering of one specific individual, Christianity made one of its most striking contributions to the understanding of humanity's deepest concerns. For it gave the highest dignity to what was more often a source of shame and despair: it took the saying of Jesus – 'Greater love has no man than this, that a man lay down his life for his friends' (John 15.13) – and said, for 'friends' read also 'enemies'. And by making one man's useless death the highest good of all, it offered to all people an identification through which all our seemingly useless suffering may be redeemed. If we can truly say, 'In Jesus I see myself', then those who are afflicted may also say, 'In this that I endure I see Jesus'. This is no easy answer, and certainly is no panacea to be dished out by those who stand on the sidelines. Its effectiveness, its truth, are only accessible to those who can take it to themselves. Nor should it be thought (and this is particularly important) that those who reject it are less worthy of respect. We are, after all, identifying just one strand of a coat of many colours. If we pull it out of the whole garment, everything may fall apart – a thought which is not inappropriate as a description of the constant ebb and flow of dialogue which is the dialectic of faith.

– 4 –

We began with a saying of Jesus to do with the nature of faith as that which constantly asks, seeks and knocks in expectation of answers. We found that in a series of examples from the scriptures of ancient Israel it was all too often the case that (at least in any obvious sense) no answers were forthcoming. This set up a contradiction of the original understanding of faith, forcing us to look more deeply at the way faith comes to grips with silence, with mystery and with the unsolvable problem of suffering. Through the insights of the Hebrew scriptures and the responses of the Christian community we have come to see that the contradiction is in its turn contradicted. There is no answer. But there are answers. We cannot say what God is like, but there is still God. To end this exploration I want now to take the next step in the process of dialectic: into the realm of faiths other than Christianity which have, like Christianity, sought by means of the light given to them to make sense of existence. If what has gone before has been sketchy, this final section must of necessity be perfunctory in the extreme. It is included not to display my woeful ignorance of the great religions of the world but to suggest (nothing more) a few directions in which the encounter between faiths might lead the individual seeker from one particular faith.

(a) If Christianity recognizes of the incarnation, the process of the divine-becoming-human, as a matter of the highest significance, might we not be able to share something of the Hindu insight of the divine-being-everything by means of which the individual's relationship to deity is explained in that religion? It is a different insight to be sure, but there is some commonality of motive: to account for the belief that there are ties between God and creation perhaps *some* such 'bridge' is needed as the Christian 'God-in-Christ' or the Hindu pantheism – 'all is God'. The parallel is closer still, of course, since Hinduism uses the concept of the *avatar* which is roughly analogous to Christianity's 'incarnation'. It means literally 'a descent', and is used of the coming of the god Vishnu in human form, most familiarly as Krishna, to communicate more directly with men and women. No doubt this concept is strictly speaking illogical, since if all is already within the divine principle, it is not meaningful to talk of the divine (or a divine being) as descending into the created realm. But then, the concept of God incarnate in a specific human individual is also completely illogical in terms of the Judaeo-Christian understanding of God as utterly transcendent. I suspect that there is much to be gained from a long-term pursuit of these themes of mutual interest.

(b) The dualistic element in certain strands of Christianity has an interesting counterpart in Hinduism. Indeed, insofar as the roots of both Zoroastrianism and Hinduism belong to a common Indo-European matrix, the connection may be more than accidental. Where Persian thought identified good and evil as two opposed and warring principles in the cosmic sphere, Hinduism sees them rather as two faces of the same reality. If good is the obverse, then evil is the reverse of the cosmic coin; in which case, of course, the moral content of the opposition between the two is removed. All that is is God, and that means that both good and bad are part of the divine whole. One of the ways in which this is symbolized is in the figure of Shiva, god of both creation and destruction. The implications of this way of thinking for the problem of suffering are obvious and considerable. What we from our Judaeo-Christian context regard as 'bad' or 'unjust' is, from a Hindu view of the world, just another aspect of what *is*. There is, however, a dialectic within Hinduism too: the theory of reincarnation regards an individual's fate in his or her present life as being determined by performance in a series of previous existences, and there is undoubtedly a moral principle at work here. Again, I cannot do more than note an area of obvious common concern here: it must be left to others to explore it in greater depth.[11]

(c) One of the central doctrines of Islam is that of the day of judgment as the time when all wrongs are righted and rewards and punishments meted out as appropriate. Like its counterpart in Christianity, this aspect of Islam assumes a heaven and hell and the justice of 'final solutions' at the end of time. Where it would be interesting for these two faiths to get together would be on the incompatibility of their teaching on *who* will be rewarded and who punished. If nothing else, such a discussion might reveal the essential injustice of both positions, and their weakness as answers to the problem of suffering. It would also lead, hopefully, to a serious examination of the teaching, again common to both, that God, that Allah, is merciful, Ar-rahim.

(d) It would be interesting to open up a dialogue on the theme of the divine plan, in which the Buddhist pattern of life with its various stages would be the other partner. Where the Christian stress is on the inevitability of what God designs, and the relative impossibility of any individual changing that design, the Buddhist emphasizes the duty of each individual to conform to the plan in order to achieve the ultimate goal of *nirvana*. Thus while the former demands subjection of the individual will to the inevitable process of God's plan for life, in order to win a place in a paradise of a very individual kind, the latter asks of each individual a voluntary striving of an intensely personal kind throughout life which will, if successful, lead to the total abnegation of all individuality and all desire in a consummation whose great attraction is that it puts an end to everything which might be regarded as process. The dialectic of such a conversation would be fascinating in the extreme, but decidedly not for the faint-hearted.

(e) Events in the twentieth century have made it impossible to talk about the meaning of suffering in isolation from the experience of the Jews and the contribution of Judaism. The sheer magnitude of the horror of the 'final solution' and the monstrous meaningless-ness of the suffering it imposed imply that we who have not shared in it must speak with reserve and with due humility on the subject of the love of God and the afflictions of the innocent. The issues which arise here have received voluminous attention in the last two decades, and there is now a dauntingly large literature on the holocaust. Yet there appears to be remarkably little recognition in Christian circles that Hitler's ultimate expression of the long tradition of anti-semitism in Christian Europe has radically altered the whole debate. It is hard now to be impressed by the martyrdom of a few individual Christians, which for all its unpleasantness was at least readily seen as having meaning; and the cross itself pales into insignificance in the shadow of Auschwitz and Dachau. There is no doubt that the theology of suffering can no longer be tackled in isolation as a purely individual matter within the bounds of a single religion: it must be pursued as a wide-ranging debate between the faiths – a debate which in truth has already begun (as even a cursory examination of the available material will reveal). It would be beyond the purpose of this very preliminary outline to offer a bibliography, but since it would be tantalizing to raise the question without at the same time offering any way into it, let me indicate a few 'starters'.

For many people their first awareness of the holocaust comes from what must now be regarded as its archetypal symbol, *The Diary of Anne Frank*. This is by no means to be despised, though it is a pity if it leaves us with a merely emotional reaction – a reaction which is of course both natural and powerful. Even such a hardened campaigner as myself found the experience of visiting the Anne

Frank Huis in Amsterdam a particularly moving one. Still at the emotional level, but with a hard edge to it, Elie Wiesel's *Night*, based on his own experiences, gives the Auschwitz horror a reflective personal dimension which compels respect and questions certainties. Then from another angle, Simon Wiesenthal's *The Sunflower* highlights by means of a telling story the moral dilemma faced by Judaism in responding to the outrages of the Nazis. What makes this book specially interesting is that a series of responses to the initial story have been included in which thinkers from a variety of religious traditions assess the moral dilemma and tease out some of the issues involved. Finally two books which are of a more academic kind, though not unengaged: Richard Rubenstein's *After Auschwitz*, and Alan Ecclestone's *The Night Sky of the Lord*, the first from a Jewish and the second from a Christian point of view.

To give the dialectic a more immediate pointedness, let me quote a story which is one of my favourites from the Hasidic legends:[12]

> Rabbi Shmelke and his brother once petitioned their teacher, the Preacher of Mezeritz, to explain to them the words of the Mishnah: 'A man must bless God for the evil in the same way that he blesses Him for the good which befalls.'
>
> The Preacher replied: 'Go to the House of Study, and you will find there a man smoking. He is Rabbi Zusya, and he will explain this to you.'
>
> When Rabbi Shmelke and his brother questioned Rabbi Zusya, he laughed and said: 'I am surprised that the Rabbi sent you to me. You must go elsewhere, and make your inquiry from one who has suffered tribulations in his lifetime. As for me, I have never experienced anything but good all my days.'
>
> But Rabbi Shmelke and his brother knew full well that from his earliest hour to the present he had endured the most grievous sorrows. Thereupon they understood the meaning of the words of the Mishnah, and the reason their Rabbi had sent them to Rabbi Zusya.

I cannot leave this note here. The latest sad twist in the dialectic of suffering is the way that certain elements of the State of Israel have appeared to become themselves users of tactics disturbingly like the weapons of the Third Reich. The Palestinians in Lebanon may have cause to complain that in the later twentieth century it is they, and not the Jews, who are the victims of a final solution. Insofar as this is a fair account (and it clearly cannot be immediately dismissed) it demonstrates forcefully the urgent need for those of faith, whatever their religion, to work out together the implications of suffering wherever it is found.

– 5 –

The subject of this chapter has been the claim that faith is not a settled or final matter; that it can best be understood as in constant dialectic with itself. One example only has been worked out in detail, beginning with a thesis drawn from the teachings of Jesus, seeing how it develops in terms of case studies from the Old Testament, pursuing it on into the Christian context by means of New Testament responses, and finally offering a few suggestions as to how we might extend the scope of the dialectic to include the insights of other faiths. I hope that this exercise has opened up some of the possibilities of this means of understanding faith: books could be written on the subject, and it may be that it will be the task of the dialogue between the faiths to write such books.

II

Worship

– I –

My original intention was to present in these last pages some theory of worship together, an attempt at a theological justification. I am convinced now that that would be both insensitive and unnecessary. If by this stage in the debate we have not been driven to pray together, no amount of theorizing will do the trick. On the other hand, those who have become aware of the inner meaning of dialogue will have been sharing in prayer for ages without being asked. They will already have felt the force of that restless and relentless spirit of God which forces from us, almost against our better judgment, the shout of acclamation, and which really does not care how we label our nominal allegiance. Sidney Carter's carol perhaps expresses it better – certainly more simply – than any theoretical discussion; indeed he 'boldly goes' one better by stepping outside the artificial confines of the speck of dust we call planet Earth. For those who still want the sober debate, the British Council of Churches has recently produced another in its helpful series of books on inter-faith issues, namely *Can We Pray Together*; but first, listen to Carter's song:

> Every star shall sing a carol,
> Every creature, high or low
> Come and praise the King of Heaven,
> By whatever name you know.
>   God above, Man below, holy is the name I know.
> When the King of all creation
> Had a cradle on the earth,
> Holy was the human body,
> Holy was the human birth.
>   God above . . .

Who can tell what other cradle,
High above the Milky Way,
Still may rock the King of Heaven,
On another Christmas Day?
            God above . . .
Every star and every planet,
Every creature, high and low,
Come and praise the King of Heaven,
By whatever name you know.
            God above . . . [1]

— 2 —

Despite what I have indicated about the naturalness of common
worship, it remains a subject likely to rouse strong feelings. While
individuals for whom dialogue has become a living reality tend to
be impatient of the very slow and cautious approach of their
parent bodies, these latter, more conscious perhaps of the dangers
than of the opportunities, see the move towards shared worship as
a dilution of the faith and a surrender to the law of the least
common denominator. This is partly a function of the difference
in perspective between those who take part and those who watch.
To the latter the shared worship may appear somewhat contrived,
a cobbling together of disparate items from here and there whose
only virtue lies in their conforming to some vaguely humanistic
expressions of minimal religious value. Insofar as this kind of
worship is effective it poses a threat, for it seems to question the
meaningfulness of the individual perceptions of particular religions, and it points in the direction of a surrender to syncretism.
While these reservations are doubtless genuine and should be
respected, they should not be allowed too much significance.
They are reflective of the hesitations of the outsider who perhaps
only half understands what is going on. From the inside the view
is rather different: what the critic sees as half-hearted humanism
may in fact be an expression, arrived at after hours of painful self-
examination, of what the several participants in dialogue share at
the deepest level of their mutual quest for understanding of and
union with the one God. 'God is love' on the lips of a hectoring,
bigoted religious rhetorician is, after all, nothing but a pious
cliche. But when spoken out of the experience of deep pain, as a
declaration of indomitable faith, it is a profound truth. Inevitably
the words are the same; it is who speaks them that makes all the
difference.

One other reservation is in order. The shared worship of which I speak is that in which a number of individuals freely participate. There are situations in which interfaith worship might take place without the express consent of all involved. In a school, for example, where there were significant numbers of Muslims or Hindus some kind of common worship might be attempted. The problems which arise in that context are different from those we have just been considering. The community is a 'captive' one, for a start, many of whom will have little or no religious involvement of any kind. Therefore the kind of points I have made about the meaningfulness of shared worship are wholly irrelevant: a quite different set of assumptions would have to be considered in the school setting. It is beyond the scope of the present study and the competence of the present writer to do this; a few pointers can be found in the booklet mentioned above, *Can We Pray Together*.[2] There is, nevertheless, no doubt that this is a crucial issue (just as is the whole area of religious education in a multifaith school) which will require active and sympathetic dialogue between schools, teachers of RE, and representatives of the various faiths.

The primary purpose of this chapter is to present a means of realizing that desire for shared worship which often accompanies dialogue. It is essentially a practical exercise. To the theoretical questions, 'Can we pray and worship together? And if so, how?', I have no further theoretical answers to give. One comment only will suffice, from the nineteenth-century Scottish dissenting minister, George Macdonald:

> 'O God!', I cried and that was all. But what are the prayers of the whole universe more than expansions of that one cry? It is not what God can give us, But God that we want.[3]

– 3 –

'Let us pray'

Which of us has not, at some time or another, listened to these words which are the formula by means of which we compose ourselves to reach out to God. Their context is public, they imply a community of worshippers, and they point to an action in which we are all together involved (and altogether involved). I would like to point to a wider community and a broader definition of that personal pronoun, which would include the prayers and the pray-ers of the whole world's reaching out to God. What follows is a miscellany (though there is a certain logic to its order) which represents one idiosyncratic and eclectic selection from the world's need to pray. The framework is roughly in tune with the Christian liturgical pattern of approach, praise, petition, response, and blessing which, though drawn from one particular tradition, has, I believe, a more general application.

In order to focus attention on the inherent relevance and significance of the individual pieces, I have deliberately refrained from identifying their origins. I believe that the value for worship any particular item may have should be recognizable without external validation. Although the collection covers most of the great religions, it is not necessarily a good thing to compose a form of worship whose primary intention is to give equal place to all faiths. A truly common approach will use those words (whatever their origin) which best express the mind and needs of the worshippers. However, the curious will find the necessary references in the appendix.

In what follows, each section begins with a passage which is by way of reflection on the theme of that section; the remaining prayers, hymns and meditations will, I hope, be found to be appropriate to the theme.

1. Approach

1   There is a story, which I hope is true, of a group of Buddhists and Christians who decided they would study the Bible together. They started, appropriately enough, with John's Gospel. 'In the beginning was the Word', was read out, and immediately an aged Buddhist monk groaned, 'Even in the beginning was there no silence in your religion?'

2   God is the Eternal One, he is everlasting and is without end. He is everlasting and eternal. He endureth for time without end, and he will exist to all eternity.

3   The Lord our God is one Lord.

4   God is love. Faith, hope, love abide, these three; but the greatest of these is love.

5   God is seated in the hearts of all.

6   There is but one God, whose name is true, the Creator, devoid of fear and enmity, immortal, unborn, self-existent, great and bountiful.

7   In every place where you find the imprint of men's feet, there
     am I.

8   In the name of God, the Merciful, the Compassionate
       Praise be to God, the Lord of the Universe,
       the Merciful, the Compassionate,
       the Authority on Judgement Day.
         It is You whom we worship
         and You whom we ask for help.
       Show us the upright way:
       the way of those whom You have favoured,
       not of those with whom You have been angry
       and those who have gone astray.

9   Blessed art thou, O Lord our God, King of the universe, who
     createst thy world every morning afresh.

10   From the unreal lead me to the real.
     From darkness lead me to light.
     From death lead me to immortality.

2. *Praise*

11   In that hour when the Egyptians died in the Red Sea the
     ministers wished to sing the song of praise before the Holy
     One, but he rebuked them saying: My handiwork is drowning
     in the sea; would you utter a song before me in honor of that?

12   How manifold are your works!
     They are hidden from the face of man,
     O sole God, apart from whom there is no other!
     You have made the earth according to your desire,
     while you were alone,
     with men, cattle and all beasts,
     everything that is on earth going on its feet,
     everything that is on high flying with its wings . . .
     The world is in your hand, as you have made it.
     When you have risen, they live, and when you set, they die,
     for you are lifetime itself; men live in you.

13   Lord of fire and death, of wind and moon and waters,
     Father of the born, and this world's father's Father,
     Hail, all hail to you – a thousand salutations.

Take our salutations, Lord, from every quarter,
Infinite of might and boundless in your glory,
    You are all that is, since everywhere we find you . . .
Author of this world, the unmoved and the moving,
You alone are fit for worship, you the highest.
Where in the three worlds shall any find your equal?

14   Praise the Lord!
Praise God in his sanctuary;
    praise him in his mighty firmament!
Praise him for his mighty deeds;
    praise him according to his exceeding greatness!
Praise him with trumpet sound;
    praise him with lute and harp!
Praise him with timbrel and dance;
    praise him with strings and pipe!
Praise him with sounding cymbals;
    praise him with loud clashing cymbals!
Let everything that breathes praise the Lord!
Praise the Lord!

15   Holy, holy, holy, is the Lord God Almighty,
    who was and is and is to come!
Worthy art thou, our Lord and God,
    to receive glory and honour and power,
for thou didst create all things,
and by thy will they existed and were created.

3. Petition

16   'Do you know . . . that I pray?'
'What for?'
'I ask God never to reveal himself to me. Because if he did I
should know that he was not God, but a liar.'

17   Who is there who has not sinned against his god,
who has constantly obeyed the commandments?
Every man who lives is sinful.
I, your servant, have committed every kind of sin.
Indeed I served you, but in untruthfulness,
I spoke lies and thought little of my sins,
I spoke unseemly words – you know it all.
I trespassed against the god who made me,

acted abominably, constantly committing sins. . . .
Enough, my god! Let your heart be still,
may the goddess, who was angry, be utterly soothed. . . .
Though my transgressions are many – free me of my guilt!
Though my misdeeds are seven – let your heart be still!
Though my sins be countless – show mercy and heal me!

18   All that we ought to have thought and have not thought;
      All that we ought to have said and have not said;
      All that we ought to have done and have not done;
      All that we ought not to have thought and yet have thought;
      All that we ought not to have spoken and yet have spoken;
      All that we ought not to have done and yet have done;
      For thoughts, words and works, pray we, O God, for
      forgiveness,
      And repent with penance.

19   Out of the depths I cry to thee, O Lord!
          Lord, hear my voice!
             Let thy ears be attentive
                to the voice of my supplications!
      If thou, O Lord, shouldst mark iniquities,
          Lord, who could stand?
             But there is forgiveness with thee,
                that thou mayest be feared.
      I wait for the Lord, my soul waits, and in his word I hope;
          my soul waits for the Lord
             more than watchmen for the morning,
                more than watchmen for the morning.

20   Our Father who art in heaven,
      Hallowed be thy name.
      Thy kingdom come,
      Thy will be done,
          On earth as it is in heaven.
      Give us this day our daily bread;
      And forgive us our debts,
          As we also have forgiven our debtors;
      And lead us not into temptation,
          But deliver us from evil.
      For thine is the kingdom, and the power, and the glory, for
      ever and ever.

21 O God, make me live lowly and die lowly and rise from the
dead among the lowly.

22 Oh Lord, forgive three sins that are due to my human
limitations.
Thou art everywhere, but I worship thee here:
Thou art without form, but I worship thee in these forms;
Thou needest no praise, yet I offer thee these prayers and
salutations.
Lord, forgive three sins that are due to my human limitations.

23 O my God! O my God! Unite the hearts of thy servants, and
reveal to them thy great purpose. May they follow thy
commandments and abide in thy law. Help them, O God, in
their endeavour, and grant them strength to serve thee. O
God! leave them not to themselves, but guide their steps by
the light of knowledge, and cheer their hearts by thy love.
Verily thou art their Helper and Lord.

24 O heavenly Father, protect and bless all things that have
breath: guard them from all evil and let them sleep in peace.

4. *Reponse*

(Since the prayers we make in response to God are very much
tied to the time and context, and to the needs of the
individuals present, almost all the pieces in this section are
comment on rather than examples of response. The one
exception is a prayer which has recently been widely recognized by people of many faiths. It is particularly relevant to
the modern world: the Prayer of Peace.)

25 Not knowing the question,
It was easy for him
To give the answer.

26 If you have two loaves of bread
give one to the poor, and sell the other –
and buy hyacinths to feed your soul.

27 Show love to all creatures, and thou wilt be happy;
for when thou lovest all things, thou lovest the Lord,
for he is all in all.

28   We are told by the Psalmist first to leave evil and then to do good. I will add that if you find it difficult to follow this advice, you may first do good, and the evil will automatically depart from you.

29   Then the righteous will answer him, 'Lord, when did we see thee hungry and feed thee, or thirsty and give thee drink? And when did we see thee a stranger and welcome thee, or naked and clothe thee? And when did we see thee sick or in prison and visit thee?' And the King will answer them, 'Truly I say to you, as you did it to one of the least of these my brethren, you did it to me.'

30   One night a certain man cried 'Allah' till his lips grew sweet
          with praising Him.
     The Devil said, 'O man of many words, where is the
     response
          "Here am I" to all this "Allah"?
     Not a single response is coming from the Throne: how long
          will you say "Allah" with grim face?'
     He was broken-hearted and lay down to sleep: in a dream he
          saw Khadir amidst the verdure,
     Who said, 'Hark, you have held back from praising God:
          why do you repent of calling unto Him?'
     He answered. 'No "Here am I" is coming to me in response:
          I fear that I am turned away from the Door.'
     Said Khadir, 'Nay; God saith: That "Allah" of thine is My
          "Here am I", and that supplication and grief
     And ardour of thine is My messenger to thee. Thy fear and
          love are the noose to catch My Favour:
     Beneath every "O Lord" of thine is many a "Here am I" from
     Me.'

31   O CHILDREN OF MEN
     Know ye not why we created you all from the same dust? That no one should exalt himself over the other. Ponder at all times in your hearts how ye were created. Since we have created you all from one substance it is incumbent on you to be even as one soul, to walk with the same feet, eat with the same mouth and dwell in the same land, that from your inmost being, by your deeds and actions, the signs of oneness and the essence of detachment may be made manifest. Such is my counsel to you, O concourse of light! Heed ye this

counsel that ye may obtain the fruit of holiness from the tree
of wondrous glory.

32 PRAYER FOR PEACE
Lead me from death to life, from falsehood to truth.
Lead me from despair to hope, from fear to trust.
Lead me from hate to love, from war to peace.
    Let peace fill our heart, our world, our universe.

5. *Blessing*

33 This religion is a raft. It takes you across a river. Only a fool
will carry the raft on his back once he has crossed. The
Buddha does not want to be worshipped. He wants you to go
along the path he shows you, to be like himself.

34 The Lord bless thee, and keep thee:
the Lord make his face to shine upon thee,
and be gracious unto thee:
the Lord lift up his countenance upon thee,
and give thee peace.

35 The peace of God, the peace of men,
The peace of Columba kindly,
The peace of Mary mild, the loving,
The peace of Christ, King of tenderness,
    The peace of Christ, King of tenderness
Be upon each window, upon each door,
Upon each entrance to the light,
Upon the four corners of my house,
Upon the four corners of my bed,
    Upon the four corners of my bed;
Upon each thing my eye takes in,
Upon each thing my mouth takes in,
Upon my body that is of earth
And upon my soul that came from on high,
    Upon my body that is of earth
    And upon my soul that came from on high.

36 God be in my head
    and in my understanding;
God be in mine eyes
    and in my looking;

> God be in my mouth
> 　　and in my speaking;
> God be in my heart
> 　　and in my thinking;
> God be at my end
> 　　and at my departing.

37　Thou art the Master; to thee I pray.
　　My body and soul are thy gifts to start life with.
　　Thou art the Father, thou the Mother, and we thy children!
　　We draw manifold blessings from thy grace.
　　None knows thy extent:
　　Thou art the highest of the high,
　　All creation is strung on thy will:
　　It has to accept all that comes from thee.
　　Thou alone knowest what informs thy purposes.
　　I am ever and ever a sacrifice unto thee.

38　Go out into the darkness
　　And put your hand into the hand of God
　　That shall be to you better than light
　　And safer than a known way.

– 4 –

The preceding makes no claims to originality, either of concept or of content. My modest hope is that some may find it useful as a starting point for their own exploration of the field of interfaith worship. But it should be acknowledged that others have been engaged upon this important work for quite some time now. The World Congress of Faiths deserves special mention. In a brief history published to mark the fortieth anniversary of the Congress (*Faiths in Fellowship*, 1976) the author, Marcus Braybrooke, reports on the development of interfaith worship since the Second World War:[4]

> On the occasion of the Coronation of Queen Elizabeth II, inspired by her request that people of all religions should pray for her, the Congress organised a special service, at the Memorial Hall, Farringdon Street, London. About six hundred people attended and this success led the Executive Committee to decide on an annual service. . . . Subsequent services have been held at churches of several denominations, including Roman Catholic,

Anglican, Baptist and Unitarian. They have also been held at Reform and Liberal synagogues. Until recently, other faiths have not possessed large enough buildings in central London for the Annual Service.

Braybrooke makes it clear that this initiative did not meet with unqualified approval; and, as a result of disapproval from a number of Christians, a report was produced[5] in which the theological rationale for such services was considered.

The report of the group suggests that those taking part believed that members of all faiths worshipped the same God, the Creator of all, and that such services witnessed to the ethical values upheld in every faith. The group rejected the view that attendance at such services implied disloyalty to Jesus Christ.

It is only when those who believe try to worship together that they discover how much or how little their dialogue has really achieved. For all the talking in the world, all the joint communiques and declarations of shared intent are rendered null and void if afterwards, when the press have departed and the cameras have gone blind, we retreat to our separate places of worship to give thanks. If we cannot share in prayer, we have not shared at all and we have once more broken in a thousand pieces the god whose oneness is at the heart of all our teaching. When Victor Gollancz and Barbara Greene chose the title *God of a Hundred Names* for their justly famous collection of 'Prayers of Many Peoples and Creeds' they found, I believe, exactly the right tone for the project: an expression of unity through diversity, of the harmony of the ultimate through the varieties of prayer. In his preface to the collection Gollancz says something which I cannot improve upon as a *leitmotif* for this brief essay in interfaith worship – and, incidentally, for the whole book:

From amidst diversified and often warring creeds: over a vast span of history: in the language of many a tribe and many a nation: out of the mouths of the learned and simple, the lowly and great: despite oceans of bloodshed, and torturing inhumanities, and persecutions unspeakable – the single voice of a greater Humanity rises confidently to heaven, saying 'We adore Thee, who art One and who art Love: and it is in unity and love that we would live together, doing Thy will'.[6]

12

Epilogue

I am both by profession and by choice a student of the Bible, in particular of that portion of it known to Christians as the Old Testament. It will be clear that, while I hold no brief for any fundamentalist or authoritarian view of its importance, I nonetheless have the highest regard for the scriptures. Throughout this study I have made regular reference to them; not (I hope) as a source of ready-made proof texts, but rather as a measure of my thinking and understanding. In a century when the rapid increase of knowledge, coupled with the limited capacity of the human mind, has threatened a whole range of 'traditional' studies which are superficially seen as being little more than a hindrance to the scientific and technological advances so highly valued by society, it may seem slightly dotty to appeal to ancient texts from the pre-scientific world. Better, surely, to shelve them in the same dusty back room which appears to have been reserved for Greek, Latin, Alchemy and Long Division. For even though a certain artificial demand remains for biblical studies because the Christian denominations still pay lip service to the idea of the authority of scripture, it is evident that this is indeed a mere convention. *Real* interest in the subject is very limited. Conservative evangelicals preserve a limited knowledge of the text insofar as it confirms their group beliefs, but rarely come to grips with it in its own right. And even this perfunctory awareness is lacking in the 'liberal' and 'radical' alternative groups which frequently degenerate into a purely politicized view of religion whose only interest in the Bible is as a source of Marxist, Ecologist or Liberationist slogans. Meanwhile the silent majority remains, as might be expected, resolutely silent, reaching for a Bible only when the table-leg seems shaky or Johnny needs one for RE at school.

My personal conviction is that even in the world of the late twentieth century (which Lesslie Newbigin has recently described as *The Other Side of 1984*),[1] the Christian scriptures have, properly understood, a continuing significance in our quest for a way of life which takes account of God. While not wishing to endorse all its detail, I would be in broad sympathy with Newbigin's concern in the book just mentioned[2] to re-establish the importance of the Old and New Testaments. He is particularly exercised by the gulf which has opened up between critical biblical scholarship and any possible lay use of scripture, but rejects the easy answer of simply ignoring the last two hundred years of academic study of the Bible.

> . . . it must be said plainly that there is no way by which the Bible can be restored to the laity by taking it out of the hands of the scholars. The results of two centuries of critical study cannot be wished away. And the layman and woman are themselves part of modern culture and cannot with integrity divide their mental world into two parts, one controlled by that culture and the other by the Bible. A much more exciting and costly move is called for, namely a genuinely missionary encounter between a scriptural faith and modern culture. By this I mean an encounter which takes our culture seriously yet does not take it as the final truth by which scripture is to be evaluated, but rather holds up the modern world to the mirror of the Bible in order to understand how we, who are part of modern culture, are required to re-examine our assumptions and reorder our thinking and acting. This is, I believe, our present task.[3]

It has been my intention in the shaping of this study of Christian dialogue to relate to the scriptures in just such a way as Newbigin advocates. I am, of course, part of the system which he implicitly criticizes. The reader must judge whether I have to any extent succeeded in what I set out to do.

It should also be stated explicitly that I belong to the Christian community, and that my aim has been to present a Christian analysis of dialogue. Therefore the stress I place on the Bible is to be understood in that context, and should not be taken to imply that other scriptures are of no importance. But for me the Bible is normative in terms of faith and life: it calls me back again and again to my roots, and offers an inspired resource with which I am in constant dialogue. At the personal level this mirrors what ought to be a constant dialectic in the church between theology and scripture. Neither discipline is sufficient in itself: would-be comprehensive systems of theology must be repeatedly challenged by

the marvellous and kaleidoscopic variety of the Bible's insights;
and the arrogance of both scholar and fundamentalist which leads
them to believe they have the last word on scripture needs the
constant presence of theology which, drawn from the direct
experience and thought of living men and women, provides a
necessary corrective to the sterility of narrow biblicism. What this
interactive process also does is to protect us from the dangers of
religious terrorism. As long as we hold theology and scripture in
tension, neither can claim absolute authority. And one of the
lessons of Ulster, Iran and Pakistan is that the threat of theocratic
dictatorship is by no means idle. There are many who would dearly
love to have the power to impose their religious opinions on us all,
and one of the best weapons against them is to encourage the spirit
of dialogue.

— 2 —

There is a saying attributed to Jesus in a number of places which
exemplifies how the Bible can both challenge and be challenged by
theology. It is found in Matthew 16.24–25 (with parallels in 10.38–
39; Mark 8.34; Luke 14.27; 17.33; John 12.25; see also the similar
saying in Matthew 23.12; Luke 14.11; 18.14):

> If any man would come after me, let him deny himself and take
> up his cross and follow me. For whoever would save his life will
> lose it, and whoever loses his life for my sake will find it.

It is clear in the first place that this saying constantly reminds us of
the lowly and self-denying rôle that we are called to as Christians.
Therefore it inevitably questions any individual who claims any
special or over-riding authority, who enjoys either special status or
material privilege within the Christian community. So far so good.
But there is a way of looking at the text in question which retreats
from the individualism of Western Christianity and brings to bear
something of the sense of communal identity which has often been
seen as a key feature of the Old Testament. What if, from a modern
conception of the interrelatedness of humanity, we challenge the
purely personal application of the saying? Might it not be argued
that what is true for each of us individually should be true of the
community as a whole? And so we return to the text, with this in
mind, to see what it has to say to us.

If we think in terms not of individual Christians, but of their
corporate identity as a church, an interesting new interpretation
becomes possible. When the church is challenged to lose its life in

order to find it, resonances are set up which call to mind things we said in Chapter 2 about the need to risk one's faith in dialogue. Could this be applied to the church as a whole? In most of its institutional forms the church appears to be aggressive and repressive, its theology more a matter of dogma than of discovery. It is constitutionally ill-prepared for dialogue. Perhaps if, following through this line of interpretation, it were to adopt a submissive and self-denying stance in the world of religions it would come closer to realizing the full extent of what Jesus meant by self-denial. Thus the text, seen in the light of a theology of community, takes on a new life and challenges us *as a church* to take a bold step into the future. There is, after all, something incongruous about a community which at one and the same time preaches self-denial to the individual but in practice exercises a highly authoritarian control. Dare we, as a church, follow our Lord in abandoning our self-esteem in favour of real life? Dialogue, after all, is a call to the community as a whole as well as to each of us individually.[4]

– 3 –

This study began with a hypothesis in the form of a question: Can we affirm both the uniqueness of Christianity and the truth of other religions? I am convinced that the Christian faith, from its own unique understanding of God as revealed in Jesus, can confidently affirm the real and important insights of other faiths. Wesley Ariarajah, in *The Other Side of 1984*, expresses it well:[5]

> It should be noted that in a dialogue no person has the right to assume that all the truth is on his or her side. This should be a warning to Christians taking part in . . . dialogue who sometimes tend to believe that, even though dialogue involves the taking of risks, the truth revealed to them is so secure that there is no real danger of its being challenged. I wish to emphasize this point because of two reasons.
>
> First to re-emphasize the fact that there can be no return to dogma as if nothing had happened. Dogma has indeed been badly mauled. We must recognize the role of reason to question dogma, without making reason the absolute arbiter. The relationship is dialectical.
>
> Also, it is important to go beyond the stage of presenting reason and faith as alternatives or as mutually exclusive authorities. In some of the Indian religious traditions there is an insistence on a cluster of authorities that mutually enlighten and correct each

other. Faith and reason, tradition and experience can in fact be held together as a cluster of authorities that shed light from various angles, enabling the mystery of life to be understood from many perspectives.

We are indeed called to go into all the world: not to take God to the unbeliever, but to share the God we know in Christ with those whose knowledge of God is different, but not poorer. In that sharing we will all be enriched, and the road upon which we all travel will lose some of its dangers as, together, we reach for a deeper knowledge both of life (the way) and its goal (the one God).

My own personal expression of that ambition is summed up in the 'map' which I set out at the beginning of this book. Let me end by restating it, in the hope that what it expresses may be understood now in the light of what has gone before, and may perhaps therefore be better understood:

> I believe that in the end human life makes sense,
> and that its meaning can be found in God.
> I believe that God is wholly other,
> the source of everything that exists,
> yet known to all who dare to look beyond their own
>   horizons.
> I believe that in Jesus, the promised One,
> there is a door open to God,
> a door that leads to a life of love and the giving of
>   self.
> I believe that Jesus shows me
>   – the oneness of God,
>   – the common humanity of all people of whatever creed,
>   colour or race,
>   – and the meaning of life together.
> This is my belief.
> It is also my hope, and my prayer.

Notes

Introduction

1. Writing in response to Lesslie Newbigin in the latter's *The Other Side of 1984*, World Council of Churches 1984, pp. 74–75.

1. My Way

1. By 'ontological' I mean to convey that the Trinity exists in a real sense, that it is not a metaphorical description of God, but a substantive expression of God's essential nature.

2. Two writers in particular have in recent years questioned the assumption that the Jews must be held responsible for the trial and crucifixion of Jesus: Paul Winter, in his *On the Trial of Jesus*, second edition, Walter de Gruyter 1974, which depends on a detailed literary and text-critical analysis of the Gospel records; and Haim Cohn, in *The Trial and Death of Jesus*, Weidenfeld & Nicolson 1972. Cohn is a lawyer, and his discussion is very much concerned with the legal status of the events behind the Gospel accounts; in particular, with what could or could not have been done under the aegis of the Roman authority. At a more popular level, see Ellis Rivkin's recent short study, *What Crucified Jesus?*, Abingdon Press 1984.

3. The Council of Chalcedon in 451 CE came at the end of a long and acrimonious period of the church's history, fraught by conflicting ideas and a bitter struggle for power between the major Christian centres. The doctrinal statements of Chalcedon therefore represent in part a compromise, and in part a definition of orthodoxy designed to impose a single theological structure on the whole church. It failed in both of these aims: the compromise was not effective, and the direct consequence of Chalcedon was the major division between the Eastern (Orthodox) and the Western (Roman) churches – a division still with us. The Reformed churches, like the Roman, are Chalcedonian.

2. Apprehensions

1. There is a conscious allusion here to the series of programmes made for BBC television several years ago by Ronald Eyre. See his book, *Ronald Eyre on the Long Search*, Fount paperbacks 1979.

2. See above pp. 1f.

3. See Paul Tillich, *Christianity and the Encounter of the World Religions*, (Bampton Lectures 1961) Columbia University Press 1963.

4. Lesslie Newbigin, 'The Basis, Purpose and Manner of Inter-Faith Dialogue', *Scottish Journal of Theology* 30, 1977, pp. 253–70.

5. R. Sundarara Rajan, 'Negations: an article on dialogue among religions', *Religion and Society* (Bangalore), XXI (4), p. 74.

6. *The Other Side of 1984*, pp. 30–31.

7. See above pp. 9–10.

8. Most notoriously, John Hick and others in *The Myth of God Incarnate*, SCM Press 1977. Recently Alan Race, in his stimulating study *Christians and Religious Pluralism*, SCM Press 1983, has argued forcefully for a new approach to the theology of incarnation in the context of world religions. See in particular his Chapter 5, pp. 106–37.

9. See above p. 10.

3. Options

1. Newbigin, 'Basis, Purpose and Manner', p. 268.

2. An expression first used, as far as I know, by Antony Flew in the now famous collection *New Essays in Philosophical Theology*, ed. Antony Flew and Alasdair MacIntyre, SCM Press 1955, p. 97. It would be hard to exaggerate the seminal importance of this volume, which has had enormous influence on the philosophical discussion of theology in the last thirty years.

3. The details of Cyrus's arrangements for the Temple in Jerusalem are recorded in Ezra 1.2–4. The historical reliability of this information is enhanced by the existence of the Cyrus Cylinder which gives us direct evidence of that king's policies towards the religions of subject peoples. The Cylinder does not explicitly refer to Jerusalem, but shows that the Decree in Ezra was part and parcel of Cyrus's approach to the government of his sprawling empire.

> . . . the holy cities beyond the Tigris whose sanctuaries had been in ruins over a long period, the gods whose dwelling is in their midst, I returned to their places, and housed them in lasting dwellings. The gods of Sumer and Akkad whom Nabonidus, to the anger of the lord of the gods, had brought into Babylon, at the command of Marduk, the great lord, I settled in peace in their dwellings, resting places of delight. May all the gods whom I have placed in their sanctuaries address a daily prayer in my favour before Bel and Nabu, that my days may be long . . .

Quoted from John M. Allegro, *The Chosen People*, Panther Books 1973, pp. 43–44.

4. *The Other Side of 1984*, p. 74.

5. *Pope Joan* is a translation by Lawrence Durrell of Emmanuel Royidis's *Papissa Joanna*, first published in 1886. My copy is a Sphere Books edition of 1971 and the incident referred to can be found on pp. 38–39.

6. Alastair G. Hunter, 'How Many Gods had Ruth?', *Scottish Journal of Theology* 34, 1981, p. 436. Alan Race, *Christians and Religious Pluralism*, pp. 1–105, examines the options presented in this chapter in much greater detail from the point of view of recent Christian theological thinking on the subject. This book is recommended to those who wish to go deeper than is possible in the present study.

4. Theory

1. Overseas Students Information Magazine for the Universities of Glasgow and Strathclyde, issue 11, January 1984, p. 3.

2. *Christians in Dialogue with Men of Other Faiths*, World Council of Churches meeting, Kandy 1967.

3. For further reading on these issues see Fritjof Capra, *The Tao of Physics*, Fontana 1976; Gary Zukav, *The Dancing Wu Li Masters*, Fontana 1980; and Robert Pirsig, *Zen and the Art of Motor Cycle Maintenance*, Corgi 1976.

4. Newbigin, quoted in Chapter 2, see p. 9 above.

5. See above pp. 10 and 16.

6. See above p. 10.

7. Newbigin, 'Basis, Purpose and Manner', p. 268.

8. Page 2 above.

9. Page 8 above.

10. *The Common Bible*, Collins 1973.

11. See above Chapter 2, pp. 11–13.

5. Exemplar

1. See above pp. 4–6.

2. See above pp. 37f.

3. Samuel Sandmel, *Philo of Alexandria*, Oxford University Press 1979, p. 91.

4. See for example, C. F. D. Moule, *The Origin of Christology*, Cambridge University Press 1977, and two books by Geza Vermes: *Jesus the Jew*, Collins 1973, second edition SCM Press 1983, and *Jesus and the World of Judaism*, SCM Press 1983. John Riches' book *Jesus and the Transformation of Judaism*, Darton, Longman & Todd 1980, is an important contribution to the study of Jesus as a man whose roots are firmly within Judaism, yet who (without denying these roots) brought about a significant change of direction.

5. Ellis Rivkin, *A Hidden Revolution*, SPCK 1979.

6. Creeds for Christians

1. *The Scots Confession of 1560*, ed. and trs G. D. Henderson and J. Bulloch, St Andrew Press 1960; S. W. Caruthers (ed.), *The Westminster Confession of Faith*, Free Presbyterian Publications 1978. The *First Article Declaratory*, being relatively brief, is here reproduced in full:

The Church of Scotland is part of the Holy Catholic or Universal Church; worshipping one God, Almighty, all-wise, and all-loving, in the Trinity of the Father, the Son, and the Holy Ghost, the same in substance, equal in power and glory; adoring the Father, infinite in Majesty, of whom are all things; confessing our Lord Jesus Christ, the Eternal Son, made very man for our salvation; glorying in His Cross and Resurrection, and owning obedience to Him as the Head over all things to His Church; trusting in the promised renewal and guidance of the Holy Spirit;

proclaiming the forgiveness of sins and acceptance with God through faith in Christ, and the gift of Eternal Life; and labouring for the advancement of the Kingdom of God throughout the world. The Church of Scotland adheres to the Scottish Reformation; receives the Word of God which is contained in the Scriptures of the Old and New Testaments as its supreme rule of faith and life; and avows the fundamental doctrines of the Catholic faith founded thereupon.

(This statement was first approved by the Assembly in 1919, and became effective in 1926.)

2. 'The Church recognizes liberty of opinion in points of doctrine other than those affirmed and avowed in the first of the Articles Declaratory . . .' *Overture Anent Amendment of Declaratory Articles*, General Assembly of the Church of Scotland 1984.

3. Things which are of the *esse* of the church are those which are necessary to its being, which cannot be dispensed with. Things which are of the *bene esse* are good, but not essential.

4. See above pp. 41–46.

5. William Barclay quotes it in full in his *Jesus as They Saw Him*, SCM Press 1962, pp. 98–100.

6. The quotation here is from George W. E. Nickelsburg, *Jewish Literature between the Bible and the Mishnah*, SCM Press 1981, p. 208.

7. I. Epstein, *Judaism*, Penguin Books 1959, pp. 139–40.

8. Vermes, *Jesus the Jew*, p. 41.

9. Page 66 above.

10. There does exist a creed (from the United Church of Canada) which seems to me to sum up quite accurately the approach of this chapter. Moreover, it has the advantage of being not just an individual – and hence idiosyncratic – statement, but an official declaration by a recognized community of Christians. It runs as follows:

> We believe in God;
> who has created and is creating,
> who has come in the true man, Jesus,
> to reconcile and make new,
> who works in us and others by his Spirit.
> We trust him.
> He calls us to be his church;
> to celebrate his presence,
> to love and serve others,
> to seek justice and resist evil,
> to proclaim Jesus, crucified and risen,
> our judge and our hope.
>
> In life, in death, in life beyond death,
> God is with us.
> We are not alone.
>
> Thanks be to God.

7. *Practice*

1. The word 'Pakistan' was coined in 1933 at Cambridge 'by a young Muslim, Choudhri Rahmat Ali, a historic achievement for which his name hitherto has been insufficiently honoured by his countrymen'. (Ian Stephens, *Pakistan: Old Country/New Nation*, Penguin Books 1964, p. 91.) Stephens goes on to quote Ali's explanation, from the pamphlet 'Now or Never' in which it first appeared:

Pakistan is both a Persian and an Urdu word, composed of letters taken from the names of our homelands: that is, Punjab, Afghania (N.–W. Frontier Province), Kashmir, Iran, Sindh, Tukharistan, Afghanistan, and Balochistan. It means the land of the Paks, the spiritually pure and clean.

2. Information about the Sharing of Faiths movement in Glasgow can be found in the following sources:

1. *Stella*, by Jessie Adamson, Kay Ramsay and Maxwell Craig, South Park Press, 20 Glasgow Street, Glasgow; 1984.
2. The tape/slide presentation, 'A World of Difference', available from the International Flat, 20 Glasgow Street, Hillhead, Glasgow.

9. *Dissonance*

1. For those who might be interested to pursue their story further there is of course a vast literature available. I will mention only one book which is a particularly well-written and balanced popular account of the missionary enterprise in Africa: Geoffrey Moorhouse, *The Missionaries*, Eyre Methuen 1973.
2. See above p. 108.
3. L. Festinger, H. W. Riecken and S. Schachter, *When Prophecy Fails*, University of Minnesota Press 1956; Robert P. Carroll, *When Prophecy Failed*, SCM Press 1979, quotation from p. 98.
4. Carroll, op. cit., pp. 86–110.
5. Festinger, op. cit., pp. 3–4.
6. Carroll, op. cit., p. 107.
7. Most strikingly in recent years has been the attack by James Barr in his comprehensive book *Fundamentalism*, SCM Press 1977, revised second edition 1981, and in *Escaping from Fundamentalism*, SCM Press 1984.
8. 'Hermeneutic' is perhaps something of a jargon word in modern literary criticism and biblical studies. It refers to the task of interpretation, of finding out the various layers of meaning that a text contains.
9. See above pp. 91–94.
10. See Chapter 3, pp. 22f. above.
11. Flew and MacIntyre, *New Essays in Philosophical Theology*, p. 96.
12. See Chapter 2 above.

10. *Dialectic*

1. See above Chapter 2, p. 11.

2. In his *Hegel* (Weidenfeld & Nicolson 1966), Walter Kaufmann argues forcefully that the association of Hegel with this formal triad of thesis-antithesis-synthesis is wholly unwarranted and a misrepresentation of Hegel's ideas. Thus on p. 168: 'Fichte introduced into German philosophy the three-step of thesis, antithesis, and synthesis, using these three terms. Schelling took up this terminology; Hegel did not. He never once used these three terms together to designate three stages in an argument or account in any of his books.'

3. In T. M. Knox and Richard Kroner, *On Christianity: Early Theological Writings*, University of Chicago Press 1948, p. 32.

4. All the quotations in this paragraph are from Robert Davidson, *The Courage to Doubt*, SCM Press 1983, p. 34.

5. See Condition 5 listed on p. 114 above.

6. The translation given here is unusual. Most versions take the Hebrew to refer to God, and translate 'your Creator'. Without going into technical detail, it is possible that the word used in fact means 'pit', a common metaphor for death and the grave in the Old Testament.

7. See almost any modern version of this passage, and note the number of alternative translations and reservations made. RSV, for example, says of verse 26, 'The meaning of this verse is uncertain'. That is certainly an understatement!

8. Jack Kahn, *Job's Illness*, Pergamon Press 1975. I would not wish it to be thought that I was dismissive of this book. Within its terms of reference it is a most interesting and stimulating study. Amongst many gems, he offers the thought (attributed to Robert Burton, though I have been unable to trace the reference) that Job's wife was sent by God as a particularly refined element of his suffering!

9. In many of the Psalms the personal pronoun *hû'* (= 'he') is used much more frequently than is normal in Hebrew, and one scholar at least has suggested that the origin of the name 'Yahweh' might be found in this liturgical usage, perhaps through the combination of some exclamation as 'Ya!' with the pronoun.

10. Other translations have 'Repent *in* dust and ashes', which of course gives a completely different meaning. My translation follows that indicated by Lester J. Kuyper in *Vetus Testamentum* IX, 1959, p. 91 and Dale Patrick, ibid., XXVI, 1976, p. 369, and much earlier, by Maimonides in *The Guide for the Perplexed*, III, 23.

11. The best discussion of this subject known to me is in John Hick, *Death and Eternal Life*, Collins 1979, a book which is a superb example of the kind of inter-faith theological discipline which I am arguing for.

12. From *The Hasidic Anthology*, translated, selected and arranged by Louis I. Newman in collaboration with S. Spitz and included in the collection by Victor Gollancz, *A Year of Grace*, Gollancz 1950, p. 227.

11. Worship

1. Sydney Carter, 'Every Star shall sing a Carol', from *Praise for Today*, Galliard, Stainer & Bell 1974.

2. *Can We Pray Together?*, British Council of Churches 1983, pp. 26–27.

3. Quoted in C. S. Lewis's anthology of his writings: *George Macdonald:*

an Anthology, Geoffrey Bles 1946, p. 110.

4. Marcus Braybrooke, *Faiths in Fellowship*, World Congress of Faiths 1976, pp. 24–25.

5. Marcus Braybrooke (ed.), *Inter-Faith Worship*, Galliard 1974.

6. Victor Gollancz and Barbara Greene, *God of a Hundred Names*, Gollancz 1962, p. 9.

12. Epilogue

1. *The Other Side of 1984*, World Council of Churches 1984.
2. Ibid., pp. 43–54.
3. Ibid., p. 47.
4. The idea upon which this exegesis is developed was suggested to me in the first instance by Freda Thomson, one of the students involved in the Inter-faith Dialogue described in Chapter 7. The ingredients which combine to form one's opinions are often anonymous and unacknowledged; it gives me pleasure, therefore, to repay just one small debt, which may stand for a great many left outstanding.
5. *The Other Side of 1984*, pp. 71–72.

Appendix

Sources of materials used in Chapter 11, pp. 151ff. Many of the quotations can be found in the collection by Barbara Greene and Victor Gollancz, *God of a Hundred Names*, Gollancz 1962, which is referred to by the abbreviation *GHN*.

1. M. Wadsworth (ed.), *Ways of Reading the Bible*, Harvester Press 1981, p. 402.
2. Old Egyptian text, *GHN*, p. 271.
3. Deuteronomy 6.4.
4. I John 4.8; I Corinthians 13.13.
5. The *Bhagavad-gita* (Hindu), *GHN*, p. 271.
6. The *Japji* (Sikh), *GHN*, p. 271.
7. The *Talmud* (Jewish), *GHN*, p. 271.
8. J. Kritzeck (ed.), *Anthology of Islamic Literature*, Penguin Books 1964, p. 42.
9. Contemporary Hebrew, *GHN*, p. 19.
10. The Upanishads (Hindu), *GHN*, p. 46.
11. Frank Herbert and Bill Ransom, *The Jesus Incident*, Futura 1980, p. 397. The quotation comes originally from the Talmudic Tractate, *The Sanhedrin*.
12. W. Beyerlin (ed.), *Near Eastern Texts Relating to the Old Testament*, SCM Press 1978, pp. 18–19. Part of Pharaoh Akhenaten's Hymn to Aten.
13. The *Bhagavad-gita* (Hindu), *GHN*, pp. 241–42.
14. Psalm 150.
15. Revelation 4.8, 11.
16. John Fowles, *The Magus*, Dell, New York 1965, p. 274.
17. Beyerlin, *Near Eastern Texts*, pp. 108–9. Akkadian invocation to an anonymous god.
18. The Zend-Avesta (Zoroastrian), *GHN*, pp. 186–187.
19. Psalm 130.1–6.
20. Matthew 6.9–13, and Christian liturgies.
21. Muslim, *GHN*, p. 61.
22. M. M. Kaye, *The Far Pavilions*, Allen Lane 1978, pp. 72–73, Hindu.
23. The Baha'u'llah (Baha'i).
24. Albert Schweitzer, a prayer for animals, *GHN*, p. 93.
25. Dag Hammarskjöld, *Markings*, Faber 1964, p. 158.
26. Hindu proverb; provenance unknown.
27. Tulsi Das (Hindu), *GHN*, p. 73.
28. Rabbi Yitzhak Meir of Ger, *GHN*, p. 175.

29. Matthew 25.37–40.
30. Jalalud-din Rumi (Muslim), *GHN*, pp. 273–74.
31. The Baha'u'llah (Baha'i).
32. Prayer for Peace, The Caravan, 197 Piccadilly, London W1.
33. *The Listener*, 6 October 1977, p. 436.
34. Numbers 6.24–26.
35. Gaelic, *GHN*, pp. 119–20. (The wording of the second line of the second stanza has been altered slightly.)
36. *The Church Hymnary* (Third Edition), Oxford University Press 1973, No. 433. From the *Book of Hours*, 1514.
37. Sukhmani, IV.8 (Sikh). From a pamphlet 'Hymns for the Conclusion of the Sikh Service'.
38. From the poem 'God Knows' in M. L. Haskins, *The Gate of the Year*, Hodder & Stoughton 1940. First published privately in *The Desert*, c. 1908.

Bibliography

(Books mentioned in the *Appendix* to Chapter 11 are not necessarily included in this list.)

Jessie Adamson, Kay Ramsay and Maxwell Craig, *Stella*, South Park Press 1984
John M. Allegro, *The Chosen People*, Granada Publishing 1973
William Barclay, *Jesus as They Saw Him*, SCM Press 1962
James Barr, *Fundamentalism*, SCM Press 1977; second revised edition 1981
— *Escaping from Fundamentalism*, SCM Press 1984
Marcus Braybrooke (ed.), *Inter-Faith Worship*, Galliard 1974
— *Faiths in Fellowship*, World Congress of Faiths 1976
British Council of Churches, *Relations with People of Other Faiths*, 1981
— *Can We Pray Together?*, 1983
Robert Calder, 'The Illogical Language of Prejudice', *Overseas Students Information Magazine*, Universities of Glasgow and Strathclyde 11, January 1984, p. 3.
Fitjof Capra, *The Tao of Physics*, Collins/Fontana 1976
Robert P. Carroll, *When Prophecy Failed*, SCM Press 1979
S. W. Caruthers (ed.), *The Westminster Confession of Faith*, Free Presbyterian Publications 1978
Church of England Board for Mission and Unity, *Towards a Theology for Inter-Faith Dialogue*, CIO Publishing 1978
Church of Scotland, *Basis and Plan of Union, 1929*: Articles Declaratory of the Constitution of the Church of Scotland in Matters Spiritual
Haim Cohn, *The Trial and Death of Jesus*, Weidenfeld & Nicolson 1972
Kenneth Cracknell and Christopher Lamb, *Theology on Full Alert*, British Council of Churches 1984
Robert Davidson, *The Courage to Doubt*, SCM Press 1983
Lawrence Durrell, *Pope Joan*, Sphere Books 1971; translation of Emmanuel Royidis, *Papissa Joanna*
Alan Ecclestone, *The Night Sky of the Lord*, Darton, Longman & Todd 1980
Isidore Epstein, *Judaism*, Penguin Books 1959
Ronald Eyre, *On the Long Search*, Collins/Fount 1979
Leon Festinger, H. W. Riecken and S. Schachter, *When Prophecy Fails*, Minnesota University Press 1956
Antony Flew and Alasdair MacIntyre (eds), *New Essays in Philosoph-*

ical Theology, SCM Press 1955

Anne Frank, *The Diary of Anne Frank*, Pan Books 1954

M. Friedländer, *Maimonides' The Guide for the Perplexed*, Routledge 1904²

Barbara Greene and Victor Gollancz, *God of a Hundred Names*, Gollancz 1962

Victor Gollancz, *A Year of Grace*, Gollancz 1950

G. D. Henderson and J. Bulloch, *The Scots Confession of 1560*, St Andrew Press 1960

John Hick (ed.), *The Myth of God Incarnate*, SCM Press 1977

— *Death and Eternal Life*, Collins/Fount 1979

Alastair G. Hunter, 'How Many Gods had Ruth?', *Scottish Journal of Theology* 34, 1981, p. 436

Jack Kahn, *Job's Illness*, Pergamon Press 1975

Walter Kaufmann, *Hegel*, Weidenfeld & Nicolson 1966

T. M. Knox and Richard Krone, *On Christianity: Early Theological Writings*, University of Chicago Press 1948

Lester J. Kuyper, 'The Repentance of Job', *Vetus Testamentum* IX, 1959, p. 91

C. S. Lewis, *George Macdonald: An Anthology*, Geoffrey Bles 1946

Moses Maimonides, *The Guide for the Perplexed*, see above: M. Friedländer

Geoffrey Moorhouse, *The Missionaries*, Eyre Methuen 1973

C. F. D. Moule, *The Origin of Christology*, Cambridge University Press 1977

Lesslie Newbigin, 'The Basis, Purpose and Manner of Inter-Faith Dialogue', *Scottish Journal of Theology* 30, 1977, pp. 253–70

— *The Other Side of 1984*, World Council of Churches 1984

George W. E. Nickelsburgh, *Jewish Literature between the Bible and the Mishnah*, SCM Press 1981

Dale Patrick, 'The Translation of Job 42:6', *Vetus Testamentum* XXVI, 1976, p. 369

Robert M. Pirsig, *Zen and the Art of Motor Cycle Maintenance*, Corgi 1976

Alan Race, *Christians and Religious Pluralism*, SCM Press 1983

R. Sundarara Rajan, 'Negations: an article on dialogue among religions', *Religion and Society* (Bangalore), XXI (4), p. 74

John K. Riches, *Jesus and the Transformation of Judaism*, Darton, Longman & Todd 1980

Ellis Rivkin, *What Crucified Jesus?*, Abingdon Press, Nashville 1984

Emmanuel Royidis, *Papissa Joanna* (1886), see above Lawrence Durrell, *Pope Joan*

Richard L. Rubenstein, *After Auschwitz*, Bobbs-Merrill, Indianapolis 1966

Samuel Sandmel, *Philo of Alexandria*, Oxford University Press 1979

Ian Stephens, *Pakistan: Old Country/New Nation*, Penguin Books 1964

Charles Templeton, *Act of God*, Michael Joseph 1978

Paul Tillich, *Christianity and the Encounter of the World Religions*,

(Bampton Lectures 1961), Columbia University Press 1963

United Church of Canada, *Confession of Faith*

Geza Vermes, *Jesus the Jew*, Collins 1973; second edition SCM Press 1983

— *Jesus and the World of Judaism*, SCM Press 1983

Elie Wiesel, *Night*, Penguin Books 1960

Simon Wiesenthal, *The Sunflower*, Schocken Books, New York 1976

Paul Winter, *On the Trial of Jesus*, Walter de Gruyter, Berlin, second edition 1974

World Council of Churches, *Christians in Dialogue with Men of Other Faiths*, Report of meeting at Kandy 1967

Gary Zukav, *The Dancing Wu Li Masters*, Collins/Fontana 1980